Why Panache That Pays?

Because you are about to make the switch from jeans to the job market.

Because college graduation is a rite of passage. It's an ending and a beginning.

Because academically you're qualified to face the world, but your college professors never taught you the nuances of social and business etiquette or the people skills necessary for survival in the workplace.

Because to outclass your competition, you need more than a speeding BMW and knowing who's who to get where you're going.

Because you can keep this handy book in a desk drawer, a briefcase, a coat pocket, or even under your pillow!

D1446177

Panache That Pays: The Young Professional's Guide:
How to Outclass Your Competition

GME Publishing Company
Saint Louis, Missouri 63131

Printed in the United States of America   First Edition

Library of Congress Catalog Card Number 96-95445

ISBN 0-9617665-1-4

Panache That Pays

The Young Professional's Guide:
How to Outclass Your Competition

Maria Perniciaro Everding

Thank you

Editor and coauthor:
Jodi Everding
of Saint Louis, Missouri

Illustrations:
Mike O'Day
of Mountlake Terrace, Washington

Cover, book design, and layout:
Nancy Baum Ohlemeyer
of Saint Louis, Missouri

To the college students and young professionals who have given me feedback, encouragement, and the assurance that there *is* a need for this book:

Michael Schaller, Sharon Davis Fenoglio, David Narkiewicz, Katie Costigan, Tracy Roberts, Tricia Goltschman, Debbie Goltschman, Ryan Kerner, Lisa Rodgers, Meghan Andrew, Phyllis Flowers, Michael Normile, D.J. Meister, Susan & Mark Stuhlmueller, John Collins, Mark Leinauer, Elaine Walker, Alison Renz, Jenny Doll, Tim & Tracy Zavadil, Kevin Kiley, Karen Fennell, Leslye Ellison, Jim Walkenbach, Katie Schroeder, Sherry Thompson, Kelly Robertson, Susan Macalady, Deanna Snyder, Michael McDonough, Kathy Ziminski and Arthur Paniagua.

Dedication

With love and gratitude
I dedicate this book

To Gerry, my husband, best friend,
and most enthusiastic supporter

To Jodi, our daughter, the friend
I couldn't do without

To the memory of my parents,
Vic and Rose Perniciaro

Panache That Pays

commercial airlines

Airplane travel brings a group of strangers into close confines for a specific length of time — that can mean trouble!

Give yourself plenty of time to get to the airport and be ready to board. A missed flight might mean missed appointments, meetings ... and business.

Make sure your carry-on bag is the correct size and holds everything you need. Have you ever been in the aisle seat and some big oaf hits you with the bag swinging from his shoulder (or was it one of the three in his hands)? Too many personal bags can overstuff the overhead compartment. You're allotted the same size space as everyone else.

If your travel requires more than a carry-on bag, it's a lot quicker to check in at the curb. Be sure your bags are clearly identified with your name and company address and be prepared to tip at least $1 per bag, if you want your bags (golf clubs, tennis racquet) to arrive when you do. Carry or wear anything valuable; don't send it.

Keep your conversation low, if you care to converse with your seatmate at all. If you don't, admit it: *"I'm working on a report,"* or *"I need to catch a few winks en route,"* or *"I planned to use this time to finish my novel."* Be careful talking to strangers; they often tell you more than you care to hear. Likewise, if you feel like striking up a conversation and your seatmate responds with a "hmm," take the hint and take a nap.

If you are working on your laptop, remember that you only have your tray table for spreading out your papers, not your seatmate's, too. Be considerate if you're on a long flight. The constant pinging of keys will drive others up the wall.

Remember, *one* drink airborne affects you like *two* when grounded.   Sometimes it's best not to imbibe at all.

Nobody likes airline food, but brown bagging it is tacky.   If you insist, make it something that's not very messy or malodorous (braunschweiger is bad news).

Feel like a rookie? You'll look like one if you monopolize the magazines, recline your seat so that the 6'5" man behind you is chewing on his knees, ask the flight attendant for a Wacky Watermelon Wobbler or some other strange drink, talk while the flight attendant is going through the safety precautions (even if you know them by heart), or try to tip the flight attendant (a dead giveaway).

If the person in front of you reclines his seat, don't aim the air duct at his head — politely ask him to sit up.

By the way, there is a perk to sitting in the middle seat: you get both of the armrests!

During business hours, dress professionally; otherwise business casual is fine.   (This doesn't mean a tank top and jeans.) Also, if you are not wearing socks or stockings, please keep your shoes on.

corporate jet

Should you be fortunate enough to be a guest on a corporate jet don't arrive on time — *be early.*   Realize that a couple of minutes of searching for your mislaid lip balm could cost the plane its clearance time (at least an hour's wait) and you a junior executive position.

There's no check-in or skycap. You have to carry your own bags. Travel light. This is not

the time to transport your pet iguana or haul hat boxes for your Aunt Hazel.

Defer to the corporate host or senior manager when boarding, then take the seat that is offered to you rather than just plopping anywhere.

Generally, refreshments are limited. Accept or decline what is being offered; don't make any special requests; and dispose of your litter.

Bring work to review or a newspaper to read. Leave the fashion or sports magazines at home; you want to show the bigwigs on board that you're a polished professional.

When your two feet are safely on the ground, thank the crew members by name and compliment them on a good flight. If the flight was not-so-good because of the weather, compliment the crew on their skill.

Drop a short note to the executive who was responsible for your being on the plane. If you become a regular on the corporate jet, as outside directors sometimes are, remember the crew with a small gift at some time during the year.

For some people one drink is *one* drink too many. The days of the four martini lunches are over (Hooray!). Some companies even have policies on drinking.

When offered an alcoholic beverage, avoid requesting something unusual, exotic, or an old college favorite. Jell-O shots are not business drinks.

If you don't drink, you'll look less conspicuous if you order tomato juice, orange juice, or club soda with lime.

It's none of your business why someone is not imbibing. No questions asked.

That cute little baby straw is really a stirrer — so use it just for stirring your drink. The stirrer is then placed on your service plate (when restaurant dining) or held in your napkin until you can dispose of it properly.

As a corporate host, you are responsible for anyone who has had too much to drink and can't drive home. If a guest arrives inebriated but has an accident on the way home, your company may be liable.

Before you take an intoxicated guest's keys and see that he or she has a way home, here are some helpful hints:

- Do not argue with drunks ... it's useless. Humor them instead. (This can be fun ...)

- Use any escape method to get away from a drunk. Their senses are so dulled they won't even notice your absence.

- Don't flirt with a drunk. This is like playing with firecrackers.

- Find another drunk so that they can enjoy each other's company.

- Too many drunks at the party? Go home (and fix yourself a drink).

"**D**on't judge a book by its cover," and "Beauty is only skin deep," are two adages that don't work in the business world. Once a first impression is made, it may take a lot of gripping (or groveling) to climb out of the hole one has dug. Clothing doesn't just protect you, it *projects* you.

Think about the statement you want to make and then present the statement you want *others* to perceive. Consider these when planning your professional look.

Fabrics, colors, and trends change. Develop your own style. If you don't know where to begin, engage the services of an image consultant, who can keep you stylish.

hairstyle: Hair should be styled to compliment your face shape. If you don't see your hairstyle in a current magazine, you need an update. Find a good hairstylist and stay current. Conspicuously dark or gray roots are taboo.

eyeglasses: Frames should compliment rather than dominate your face. Tinted lenses indoors make you look suspicious!

accessories: Quality is the name of the game. Don't be stingy when purchasing a briefcase, wallet, pocket calendar, business card holder, or pen set; their price is worth the statement they make about you. Briefcases, business card holders, and wallets should be strictly leather.

pens: An artillery of pens, with or without names of hotels, other companies, banks, and free giveaways is not necessary. You can use only one writing instrument at a time; let yours speak well for you.

suits: A properly fitted suit of natural fibers is a necessity. That's right, natural fibers, not 100% polyester. (Let *Saturday Night Fever* rest in peace.)

Your clothes should convey that you feel your job is important. Your clothes communicate your aspirations and are a deliberate indication of your life style. Maybe you've come a long way, but does it show?

specifically for men ...

shirts: Send your shirts to a good shirt laundry. A man's shirt collar should be loose enough to insert one finger between his neck and collar. A monogram should be subtle, match the color of the shirt, and therefore not be jumping out at others. Cuffs should be approximately 1/2 inch longer than your jacket. If you prefer French cuffs, the cuff links should be tasteful, not big and gaudy. Avoid short sleeves with a jacket. In fact, unless you're managing a fast food restaurant, avoid short sleeves with a tie.

jackets: Go for quality. Don't wear the same suit or jacket two days in a row. Next to quality is proper fit. No wrinkling across the back or under your collar. The jacket skirt should cover your rear end. The sleeves should end at your wrist. Button your jacket when standing.

trousers: Should have a slight break in front and smooth fitting pockets and pleats. If the seat is baggy, get thee to a tailor. If it's tight or any part of you bulges over the waistband, you need a tailor *and* a fitness trainer.

ties: A man's tie makes a personal statement. A tie should end at the top of the belt line. The tie width should be the same as the lapel width. Don't skimp on a tie or let anyone else buy it. Only silk ties will do. Hula girls belong in Hawaii. Beer cans and cartoon characters belong on posters and greeting cards.

belts: Your belt should be leather, classic, and simple. Avoid ornate buckles. Buy the best you can afford.

socks: Color should match slacks or shoes and go all the way over the calf (no skin showing). Argyles, like needlepoint belts, are for casual wear.

shoes: Again, buy the best quality leather you can afford. Dark colors are best. Keep them polished! (Hint: shoe shine stand at the airport) No run down heels. Laced shoes are more stylish than slip-ons.

braces: Suspenders are acceptable as long as they button inside your trousers and you don't wear a belt, too.

pocket scarf: Does not match but complements tie.

trench coat: Tan colored and belted. An all-weather coat will travel well, too. No ski jackets for business.

overcoat: Wool or cashmere, double breasted or traditional style. Best colors are tan, dark gray, or navy.

watch: Metal bands are okay, but thin, leather bands are the best. Beeping sports watches are not for business. Roman numerals are classic.

jewelry: Less is better — wedding, class, or signet ring only. No earrings, necklaces, or bracelets in the office.

specifically for women ...

There was a time when women felt that they had to dress like a man to be successful. Not any more.

color: Use colors to balance your appearance. Dark colors recede; light colors enlarge. Place these where they work to enhance your height or size.

lines & designs: Use lines and designs to give an optical illusion — again in your favor. Horizontal lines broaden, vertical lines heighten, and anything asymmetrical is the most flattering. A horizontal line worn below the waist will make you appear shorter. A horizontal line above the waist will give the illusion of height.

blouse: A woman's blouse should be silk or silk-like polyester (yes, polyester ... with the emphasis on *silk-like*), or cotton (the cloth of champions). Blouses can make a boring and dull outfit fun and fantastic. Cleavage should show only on your time.

jacket: Should be the proper fit, quality fabric, and right style and length for your figure. If your wear a lot of jackets, be sure they are mix and matchable.

skirt: The most professional skirt is a slim, simple skirt, whether it's A-line, pleated, or straight. It's a great partner for various jackets.

hemline: There are three perfect hemlines for every woman — above the knee, below the knee and below the calf. Note the three places where your leg naturally curves in. Your hemline should end at one of these to give the illusion of slimness above it.

dresses: A solid colored, fully lined chemise is best for dressing up or down.

belts: Belts go from single to multiple, from narrow to wide, from cheap to quality. String belt loops should be removed from the sides of a dress. Self-belt loops on a dress, skirt, or slacks mean you must wear a belt. Choose leather belts about 1-1/2" in width. Buckles should be gold or silver, and small. For spring and summer switch to natural, neutral tones or rope, linen, or hemp. A chain belt also may be worn day or evening. A belt that's too tight emphasizes hips.

scarves: Make scarves a part of your accessory wardrobe. Dots, checks, and plaid scarves bring energy to your looks. You can use busy scarves as sashes. Experiment with scarves. Practice tying and wearing them different ways. Be creative.

shoes: Sandals or extremely high heels should be avoided. A leather, closed-toe shoe with a comfortable heel is best. Black shoes don't go with everything. In order to elongate the body, shoes should not be lighter or brighter than your hemline.

stockings: There are numerous colors and patterns out there. Dusty colored stockings are more flattering than clear, paisley, and brightly colored pantyhose, which have no place in the office. Stick to control top pantyhose for business.

jewelry: Nothing expresses a personality as much as jewelry. Earrings, necklaces, bracelets, rings, and pins should be coordinated as carefully as the rest of a woman's wardrobe. A cheap piece of jewelry will make a very expensive outfit look cheap, but a quality piece of jewelry will make a not-so-expensive outfit look good. Keep proportion in mind. Pearls are always appropriate. Faux stones are for evening; real stones are for anytime.

A bed and breakfast is just that. A bed for the night with breakfast in the morning. It's a traditional country inn where you can nod off to the chimes of the grandfather clock and awake to the aroma of bacon in the morning.

B & Bs are cozy alternatives to the cookie cutter hotel rooms. Some offer living rooms and parlors that are used as common areas for cocktails and socializing and are more comfortable than the forced atmosphere of a hotel bar.

> " remember ... don't tip the B&B owners "

You will sit down to a home cooked breakfast in the morning. If the owners serve you, do not tip; however, you may leave a tip in your room for anyone else that serves you. (Or you can simply indicate the tip on your bill when you leave.)

B & Bs are seeking more corporate business by charging competitive rates, offering planned conference facilities, and providing business equipment.

Many young people are choosing to drink beer with meals in place of wine. Beer generally goes better with hearty, casual meals rather than elegant, delicate, or lighter meals.

Should an executive order a cocktail or wine, and your drink of choice is beer, go ahead and order one.

In college you probably drank an inexpensive beer (taste was not your motive). Now it's time to upgrade your taste buds. In a fine restaurant, you might request a certain brand or ask what they have on draft.

> " now it's time to upgrade your taste buds ... ask what's on draft "

Nix the fact that in college you could do more keg stands than anyone else. Drink beer from a glass.

When a close friend, relative, or business associate has lost a loved one, it is a very difficult time not only for the bereaved but also for those who wish to express their sympathy. It's hard to commit the "right words" (if such things really exist) to paper and even harder to comfort a mourner in person. Although we cannot bring the deceased back to life (I'm speaking for myself, of course) or truly ease the pain, keep the following guidelines in mind when writing a note of condolence or visiting a funeral home.

■ Acknowledge the loss: *"I was so sad when I heard ... "*

■ Express your sympathy: *"I'm thinking of you; I'm so sorry ... "*

■ If you knew the person, note special qualities about them or recount a memory (good, of course): *"I will always remember ... "*

■ Be sincere. Unless the very same situation has occurred in your life, avoid, *"I know how you feel"* because you don't know how the person feels.

Write a condolence note to the bereaved person to whom you were the closest.

If you're going to the funeral home because a co-worker has died and you don't know any of the family, go up to the bereaved (the person usually standing closest to the casket) and introduce yourself. After expressing your sympathy, you may be seated for a few minutes or leave. Be sure to sign the guest book first.

Death notices are in the local newspapers and state the funeral home, viewing times, services, and the family preferences for donations. If the obituary notice states that the funeral or interment is private, do not ask to attend. Companies generally have guidelines for flowers or donations in memory of a deceased person.

Appropriate dress for visiting a funeral home is professional business. No shorts, jeans, or tennis shoes.

Traditionally when an invitation stated "black tie" it meant exactly that, a *black* tie. Today, it just means formal. There are two kinds of men's formal wear: "black tie" or dinner jacket, and "white tie," which is only for the most formal occasions or old Fred Astaire movies.

The occasions to which you may wear a tuxedo are no longer limited to proms or weddings. It's perfectly acceptable these days to wear a tuxedo to the theater, opera, ballet, or even dinner at a top restaurant (you know, the kind with cloth napkins). People around you will think that you're on your way to or from an even swankier affair. (Don't wear your tuxedo virtually *everywhere*. People will catch on. At your age, there aren't *that many* swanky affairs.)

What a woman wears to a black tie gala depends on the custom in her community. It may be anything from a short dinner or cocktail dress to a long lavish gown to a string bikini and a ski mask. (There's always that *one* community ...)

Are tennis shoes permitted with a black tie? Only if the invitation says so. Otherwise men should stay with thin black dress socks and serious (stuffy?) black shoes.

" tuxedos are for more than proms and weddings "

"Black Tie Optional" allows you to wear dressy instead of formal clothing.

Don't dress below the level set by the invitation. If it reads "black tie"; don't wear your navy blue suit. Check with your companion so that one of you isn't sporting tails and the other cutoffs.

Everyone likes his or her space. Stay out of other's faces. Keep at least an arm's length away.

Good posture tells the whole world you are confident and feel good about yourself. Keep your nose in the air at a friendly angle and your chin parallel to the floor. Rounded shoulders and head down invite others to walk all over you.

Look interested (sometimes it's difficult) in what someone is saying. Crossed arms can give a bored or disagreeable impression.

Avoid bobbing your knees up and down, crossing and uncrossing your legs, tapping your toes, or cracking your knuckles. If you have a nose twitch or any other jerky habit, get rid of it.

Smiling is universal ... and contagious. Begin your day with a smile in the mirror

and you set off on a high note. Smiling makes you feel happier and the smiles that follow come faster and easier. A generous smile can help you manage in the most difficult situations.

Smile often — it also improves your face value!

A business card may be used for more than just telling people who you are and where you can be reached. It may be used as a forwarding agent — attached to a newspaper, magazine article, annual report, or any other piece of information you think might be of interest to someone. It may also be used as a gift enclosure with a personal business gift.

To personalize your card, write a short note across the front of it and sign only your first name.

Be selective about handing out your business cards. Throwing them from a bus window or scattering them around the room tells everyone that you're probably trying to sell something (like your sanity). People will avoid you.

To avoid being overly aggressive, wait until a senior executive asks for your card. Be discreet when handing someone your card, especially at a house party. Avoid bringing out your business card during a meal *("Will you please pass the beans and the business cards, Harry?")*

When you attend a meeting outside your office, hand your business card to the receptionist, but wait for someone else in the meeting to initiate an exchange.

Present your card with your name facing the person. It's better *not* to give someone your card rather than give one that is soiled, torn, or outdated. In other words, don't scratch out the last person's name and print yours in, or white out a cocktail sauce stain from the last party. An apology won't help.

Keep your cards in a quality leather card holder rather than pocketed in your wallet. Avoid putting your photo on your card, unless you provide the picture frame, too.

Don't leave home without your business card; it's the handshake you leave behind.

Many companies have adopted what is known as "casual day." The concept is to don professional business attire, but be somewhat casual. Does this mean you can wear blue jeans, green jeans, black jeans, or no jeans? Next question. Do my Dockers have to be ironed or is the wrinkled look okay?

Many people like to stretch the rules, while others simply make up their own. Every company has its own definition of business casual. Some companies have cut pictures from fashion magazines and put them into a handy book format, so that there will be no questions about exactly what business casual entails.

Casual clothing should make you look and feel good. Beyond that, it should be appropriate for the workplace.

business casual continued

To be safely conservative, this is business casual:

for men

Slacks and a polo shirt, sweater, or open-collared (keep gold-chained medallions and Brillo pad chest hair to a minimum) business shirt; polished loafers and socks (a must)

for women

Slacks with a sweater, blouse, or coordinated top; walking shorts (end at the knee) and coordinated jacket; coordinated skirt outfits; flats (coordinated, of course)

Casual *doesn't* mean warm up suits, tee shirts with advertising slogans, tennis shoes, cutoffs, Birkenstocks, tennis skirts, halter tops, biker shorts, unshaven face or legs, messy hair, and no makeup. Neatness and cleanliness are still the most important elements of casual dressing.

> " do I have to iron my Dockers? "

18

Going on the road with your boss? The person who owns the car drives it. Don't jump behind the wheel of your supervisor's new Corvette, regardless of your Autobahn aspirations or past driving record. If you're renting a car, take your eye off that Infiniti, unless you have an unlimited expense account.

When you are in the driver's seat, avoid heating up over traffic jams or road hogs. Complaining, cursing, and losing your composure show you're unable to handle stressful situations (not a good characteristic to present to your boss).

Don't smoke or raise your voice in the car. Avoid taking two spaces when parking. Should you borrow anyone's car, return it clean, *on time,* and with a full tank of gas!

Speaking of clean, would you consider having a client to your home if the floors were trashed, the windows were smudged, and gum and straw wrappers were between

the cushions of your couch? Most people would answer no (the others would just roll over and belch in reply); however, some of these same people (the ones who like to present a tidy house) don't care how their car looks when they pick up a client.

It's hard to be in the professional frame of mind (or prove that you have a frame of mind, period) when your steering wheel is sticky from

> " ———
> **a spotless car can reward you tenfold**
> ——— "

sloppy Slurpees, or your passenger (hopefully not your boss) is straining to keep his Cole-Haans off your mud-caked car mats.

A spotless car can reward you tenfold. It makes a wonderful first impression when you are taking clients out to dinner or picking them up at the airport. Your car is a reflection of you, so it might be time to wipe it with Windex.

All jokes aside, how many times have you been greeted at the airport with, "Don't mind my car. It's a mess, and I haven't had time to clean it?" Make time. Find a car wash and frequent it. (Most car washes have packages you can purchase that make it worth your while to have your car cleaned often.) Even if you don't carry others in your car, the personal benefits of having a clean car are worth the trouble it takes to clean it. You'll feel organized, clean, and efficient behind the wheel of a tidy mobile — and there's no risk of seating yourself on a stray fry (those greasy little devils) and soiling your suit in the process.

Today's technology lets you be reached quickly, no matter place or time. You can take the office with you wherever you go; even Calgon can't take you away anymore.

Cellular phones are another way to disturb and disrupt the lives of those around you. Trust that other diners aren't staring in awe of your obvious importance upon receiving a call over hors d'oeuvres, but instead glaring at your ostentatious ignorance in taking a call at a restaurant, disturbing not only the party you are eating with, but also those seated around you.

Leave your phone in the car while at the movies, a concert, a restaurant, and a church service. Even The Higher Powers don't appreciate being put on hold while you take a call.

If you absolutely *must* take a call during such a commitment, at least go to the lobby or the rest room, or somewhere you won't disturb others.

When receiving a call from your mobile unit, answer with your first and last names. This will end a call to the wrong number before it even begins. When you're calling someone on a mobile unit, after identifying yourself, ask if it's a good time to talk. You never know who the captive passenger may be.

Champagne (pale, sparkling wine) is the traditional bubbly beverage for toasting and celebrations. Buy the best champagne you can afford! Brut (Broot) is the driest designation for champagne; it denotes a fine wine with no added sugar.

If you're a novice, here's how to uncork a bottle:

■ Take care to point the bottle away from mirrors, vases, windows, and anyone's face.

■ First, untwist the wire and slip it off the cork. Remove the metal disk over the cork.

■ Now, holding the bottom of the bottle against you (and pointing the mouth of the bottle away from the crystal), slowly turn the cork, easing it up with your thumbs or giving it a quick twist with your fingers.

■ Once you become adept at it, you won't even need a towel around the neck to soak up the spillage.

Today's champagne glass of choice is the slim, tulip-shaped glass, which is held by the stem.

Has your circle of friends begun the baby picture swap meet? Maybe it's time to think about children ... Wait! Don't put the book down! We're not talking conception, just children *in general*.

How do you relate to other people's children? If you don't have children, conversing with a child may be more tedious than parleying with the parole board. Here are a few pointers:

■ Children aren't interested in your younger years unless you starred in a movie or robbed a bank (and even then, it had better be good).

■ Children don't want to discuss school, because most of them don't like school. Ask them about something they're interested in, such as sports teams or movies.

■ Telling a child how much he or she has grown will make them squirm; cheek pinching is out of the question.

If you're a parent, remember that although your children are a big part of your life, they aren't as exciting to everyone else. Before you pull out your "brag book" at a cocktail party, be assured your boss really isn't interested in how much Sammy sleeps, which soy formula gives Georgie gas, or how many presidential middle names Nancy knows. An invitation that really includes your children will have their names on it.

A baby-sitter can make an evening more enjoyable for everyone — especially your children.

class (klas), n. the ability to make people from all walks of life feel comfortable.

No one is born with class; it has to be learned and earned.

Often in a luxury hotel, not far from the registration desk, you'll see a friendly individual situated behind a desk with "concierge" on its nameplate.

The concierge *knows all* and can *do all* to help you with anything from dinner reservations to a baby sitter. He or she is then tipped on the service

"——————

the concierge knows all and can do all ...

——————,,

provided. Should the concierge get you tickets to a sold out performance, tip at least 10% of the ticket costs. If the concierge performs several services for you and gets to know you by name, tip several dollars when you leave.

Business talk is not "small talk." Have you ever watched a real conversationalist go into a room of strangers and come out with a room of friends? Ever wonder how it's done? The secret is having the desire to communicate, an interest in others, a relaxed but positive attitude, charisma, and knowledge. Here are some do's and don'ts:

do

- use new words (Branch out; expand your vocabulary!)
- compliment people
- ask questions (As long as they're not rude or intrusive; inheritances and hairpieces are off limits!)
- speak slowly and clearly
- say what you mean (and mean what you say ...)
- have good eye contact
- establish common ground *("Kate mentioned that ...")*

don't

- use jargon, slang, or trendy phrases (Jargon is to communication what paint by number is to art.)
- gossip (unless it's good gossip — and if it's good, is it really gossip?)
- preach (unless you do it for a living)
- burst someone's bubble *("Sorry, but it's been proven that the world is round!")*
- interrupt
- talk the loudest or the fastest
- go into great detail *("After they made the incision, they used the scalpel to slice the cyst off ... ")*
- finish another's sentence
- complain *("Oh, these blasted bunions! And I thought my corns were bad ... ")*

don't (continued)

■ monopolize
■ flaunt vocabulary *("It's egomaniacal effrontery, if you know what I mean?")*
■ discuss a worn out subject
■ correct others *("Didn't you mean to say 'circum scribe' there, Jack?")*
■ humiliate others
■ drag stories and jokes on and on
■ discuss weighty matters *("But what about Mill's view of duty — as opposed to Kant's, that is ... ")*
■ quote the front page of the <u>New York Times</u>
■ try to be funny, unless you are a comedian
■ discuss your children *("Little Joey still can't have liquids after eight-thirty ... ")*
■ discuss your latest diet. No one cares what your cholesterol level is.
■ argue. Rarely does anyone win.

A polished professional avoids speech tics: "ya know"; "something like that"; "like"; "well"; "um"; and gets rid of his local accent: "y'all"; "ma'am"; "hey man"; "honey doll"; or "sweetie".

If your response to most statements is "huh," you belong to the "huh" club. Drop your membership.

Record your voice sometime when you're talking on the telephone and then count your speech tics. You might be surprised.

Learn to enunciate and pronounce words properly, avoid: "git"; "spayded"; "youse"; and "boughten".

The last sound in a word is as important as the first. Rather than "doin'," or "goin'," say "doing" or "going".

A bore tells more than you want to know about diet, job, vacation, wealth, operation, sport, etc.

If you feel like you've been boring someone, STOP and admit what you've done: *"I've been doing all the talking, how do you feel about ... "*

What do you do with someone who is boring? If the situation permits, just introduce him or her to someone else.

Say what you mean and question anyone who makes an unclear statement: *"Do you mean 8:00 a.m. or p.m.?"* Communication is when others think you said what you think you said.

The quality of your voice is important. If you have a high-pitched, squeaky voice, the kind that makes dogs run away howling, try reading aloud something long and boring to practice toning down a bit.

If you know you have a monotone voice, read nursery rhymes with a lot of exaggeration. (Alone, of course.)

Read the newspaper headlines and the first and last paragraphs of the stories. You will be informed enough to ask questions such as, *"What do you think about ... ?"*.

"—— communication is when *others* think you said what *you* think you said ——"

Another great way to begin a conversation is to ask questions. *"Where are you from ... ?"* Then elaborate.

A good conversationalist can discuss anything from dogs to delicatessens — and *enjoy* doing it.

Each corporation has its own culture, its own personality, its own business ethics within the organization or industry. The only way to work within a company or industry is to abide by its rules.

> "———————
> **business is a game ... you play by the rules or you lose**
> —————,"

Corporate cultures in America are pyramidal. They operate from the top down, so business etiquette is based on hierarchy and power.

Business is a game. You play by the rules (and maybe get pulled up the ladder) or you lose.

The moral of the story: Be aware of your company's culture and don't try to beat the system.

A handwritten note is like a ray of sunshine in this haze of electronic conveniences. Unlike a telephone call, a letter is a written record and may be copied and read to others (so take heed).

Corporate letterhead is used for business correspondence only. Don't use both sides of your letterhead; instead, include a second sheet that matches your letterhead. If you want your letter to really strike people, Keep It Short and Simple (KISS).

The low man on the totem pole should be leery when sending correspondence to senior management without his or her supervisor's permission. Senior management likes to rub elbows with (and almost exclusively with) senior management. (You will, too, someday.)

Don't use corporate letterhead for:

■ personal correspondence

■ love or condolence letters

■ political fund raising

■ lawsuits

■ letters to the editor

For congratulations, appreciation, condolence, good luck, and similar types of correspondence, a handwritten note gives a personal touch and is quite memorable. Dark ink looks professional.

All correspondence deserves an honorific *or* a title, but not both. The exception is when you don't know the correct title or honorific.

If you can't find it by calling the company, address the correspondence with first and last name, such as *"Pat Jones"*, using the salutation, *"Dear Pat Jones"*. If you're clueless who will be reading your letter, use the salutation, *"Dear Reader"* instead of, *"Dear Sir or Madam"* and *"To Whom It May Concern."* They're outdated.

Being overly friendly or cute in the salutation of your letters is unprofessional. Use Mr., Ms., or Dr. until you're told to call the person by his or her first name.

Close your letters with *"Sincerely"* unless you're writing to the President of the United States or a high church official, then use *"Respectfully yours."*

Always, always, always sign your typed letters, *in ink*. If you have an androgynous name, please type (not sign) Mr. or Ms. in the signature block. Your correspondents will be grateful.

Your signature should be legible enough to serve as your identified legal mark.

You may choose your friends but *not* your co-workers. You will spend more of your waking hours with co-workers, the very people who may have nothing more than the same employer in common with you. Begin and end your day at the office by greeting those you see; a smile goes a long way. Learn to listen to others' ideas instead of trying to flaunt your recently acquired (and probably not yet fully paid for) knowledge. Avoid being judgmental about who's who in the company hierarchy. (You've heard the stories about mail boys becoming chairmen of boards.)

> " **when you're new ... everyone will be checking you out** "

Being popular at work is great, but keep your priorities straight and do not jump immediately into a frenzied quest for friends. When you're new to the company, everyone is going to be checking you out, so you might as well take your time in sizing up your co-workers, too. Everyone will not become a close friend and that's OK!

Don't ask about or get involved in anyone's personal affairs. Take any grapevine garbage to the trash can. Be diplomatic and noncommittal.

You have to get along with your co-workers (if you want to remain their co-worker, that is). If there's someone you really don't see eye to eye with and you're ready to explode

— *don't*. Instead, find another way to vent your feelings: build an effigy out of paper clips, or write the person's name on the sole of your shoe.

If applicable, do your fair share of making coffee, cleaning out the filter, rinsing out the coffee pot and your dirty cup. Leave the kitchen or lunchroom tidy. Don't swipe anyone's lunch from the refrigerator.

Let your co-workers know when you need their help. Avoid placing unrealistic demands on a subordinate, or asking someone to do something that you wouldn't do yourself. Never command or demand. There's a difference between being a boss and being bossy. The most important words in business are "please," "thank you," and "I'm sorry." Use them.

there's no "I" in "team"

Personal affairs are not business promotions. Don't let Cupid be stupid; keep your personal life separate from your professional life.

You have a choice in where you want to work. So, if you don't like your job, find another one. You represent your company at all times (even on the weekends at your old college hangout). Badmouthing your employer or ripping on your company policies makes you look foolish.

There's no "I" in team and commitment is the glue that holds the team together. Be committed and be a team member. Or, look for employment elsewhere.

diet

This four-letter word seems to be on the lips of many diners, but it's rude, rude, rude to discuss dieting during a meal.

You can offend and infuriate a host or hostess by commenting on the fat of his or her fried wontons, or by insisting on eating only the cancer-fighting veggies that aren't part of the meal.

Don't comment on how many croutons equal one bread, how many daily grams of fiber keep you regular, how much fat is in the salad dressing, or why you get those itchy hives from anything chocolate (obviously why you're declining dessert).

" **try not to make others self-conscious** "

Try not to make other people self-conscious about what they're eating *("Do you know what that poor cow had to go through?)* and observe your own eating habits in silence.

A unt Mildred once said, "You never really know someone until you have them to your home for dinner." Your table manners can make or break you. Follow these do's and (especially) don'ts:

do

■ sit up straight, but not stiffly. Your forearms may rest on the table (if there is room) and your elbows may also rest there in between courses.

■ put your napkin on your lap. Use it. Place it on the table, *not* the chair, if you have to get up during a meal.

■ wait for your host or hostess to begin eating or give a similar green light to begin.

■ serve food from the left and remove from the right.

■ bring the food to your mouth, *not* your mouth down to the food.

■ pass *both* the salt and pepper when some-one asks for just one.

■ pick up a dropped utensil at someone's home if you can do so without putting your head in the spinach. (Surely the hostess will notice and get you a clean one.)

■ say "No, thank you" when declining food, rather than questioning, "Is the sauce sup-posed to be green?"

■ remove a seed, an olive pit, a bone or a piece of gristle from your mouth with your cupped fingers. Hide it under something on your plate, not on the table. (Now you know why parsley is on the plate.)

■ blot your lips with your napkin before taking a drink. Lipstick and "whatever" on your glass is offensive.

- wipe your nose at the table, if necessary, but *never* on your napkin. However, if you have to really blow the foghorn, excuse yourself and go to the rest room.
- eat finger foods with your fingers, but then use your napkin because *nothing* is finger lickin' good (all apologies to the Colonel).
- offer to help clean up something you've spilled, but don't embarrass everyone by being overly apologetic. (The host or hostess knows where to find you.)
- food that flies off your plate onto the table should be retrieved with your fingers and put on your plate, not in your mouth.
- drink water if something is too hot, as opposed to spitting it out, screaming, or fanning your open mouth with your hands.

don't

■ use your water glass as a finger bowl or take ice from it to cool soup, coffee, or tea.

■ slurp or blow on your soup. It is okay to put crackers in it as long as they're not completely mashed.

■ crunch the ice in your drink or chomp on hard candy.

■ push your plate away or stack your plates when you have finished eating.

■ talk with food in your mouth or eat, drink, and talk at the same time. (Heard this before?)

■ chew with your mouth open.

■ use a toothpick. If you have something lodged between your teeth, drink water. If it still won't dislodge, proceed to the rest room.

■ apply or touch up makeup.

■ apologize for not eating something. What you eat is your choice.

■ use your utensil as a serving utensil and don't put a serving utensil in your mouth.

■ put a utensil on the table once it has been used, place it on a plate.

■ ask for anything you don't see. Asking for catsup to put on your prime rib (when it's not on the table) will insult your hostess.

■ blow out the candles, unless they're on your birthday cake, of course.

In spite of everything you've just read, RELAX. Should you still commit a dining gaffe have the confidence to laugh at yourself and the class to ignore anyone else's rudeness.

Success in today's workplace relies upon dealing with a variety of people, including those who have disabilities. If someone in your office has a disability, it may become *your* handicap if you don't know how to deal with him or her properly.

■ Use the term "disabled" instead of "handicapped."

■ Put the person before the disability. For example, "person with a disability."

■ Although people may have physical disabilities, this does not mean that they are not as able as others to carry on business.

■ Don't offer to push someone's wheelchair or guide someone by the arm. Uninvited assistance can be insulting.

■ For the hearing impaired, speak slowly and clearly, but don't overenunciate. If a sign language interpreter is present, speak to the person with the hearing impairment, not to the interpreter.

■ For those with visual impairments, use their names when addressing them.

■ Discuss people's disabilities *only* at their discretion.

■ Avoid speaking loudly to someone with a disability other than hearing impairment.

■ Always focus on people's interests and abilities. These, not their disabilities, are what define them as people.

O h yes, we know ... it's really for your dog, but that's not the point.

As the corporate host, you don't ask for a doggie bag. Even if the guy across from you skipped out early, don't claim his leftovers just because you're footing the bill.

Should you be someone else's guest, it won't impress anyone (especially a superior) if you ask for a doggie bag.

If it's strictly a personal dinner, each paying for his own, then you may ask for a doggie bag, but forget tossing in a few rolls, some butter, and a set of stainless flatware.

Unless you suddenly find yourself in a black and white movie, it isn't necessary to follow the age-old rule, "guy opens door for girl." The first one to the door opens it.

It's always a smart move to open the door for the corporate president or chairman of the board. Allowing someone else to go ahead of you is a sign of

> " common courtesy is still alive and well "

courtesy and respect, whether the person is the janitor or the CEO. (Both deserve your respect.)

A host goes through a swinging or revolving door first so that he or she can direct the others.

If you're in doubt about opening a door for a woman, ask first: *"May I get the door for you?"* Should she prefer to open it herself, it may save you from getting smacked in the head for being thoughtful.

If you are a woman and a man opens a door for you, express your appreciation. The chances are pretty good that he knows you can do it yourself.

Always open the door for someone who has his or her hands full. Chivalry ended when King Arthur sold his last share, but common courtesy is still alive and well.

Think before you e-mail! Many people have suffered repercussions from what they have e-mailed because *nothing* is confidential or personal once it has been sent electronically. Don't put anything on e-mail you couldn't say to someone's face.

E-mail is an easy and speedy way to communicate between offices, within an internal network, or to an external e-mail system via a modem. Take advantage of the speed of e-mail but beware of becoming too informal or careless.

Message headers provide the date, time, and name of sender, so you don't have to bother with that, but it sure is nice to use a salutation ("Dear Bill:") and a closing ("Best regards,") to warm up a cold, mechanical note.

> **"*nothing* is confidential when sent electronically"**

Use a reference line. For lengthy messages, or anything important, follow up with a hard copy. Avoid using foul language, incorrect grammar, or misspelled words. Compliment, rather than insult or ridicule, someone.

With our electronic modes of communication, we could go for days without speaking to another human being, but it's good manners and consideration of others that put humanity back into the workplace.

Some companies permit employees the convenience of snacking and drinking at their desks.

Be sensitive to your co-workers when exercising such a privilege. Don't bring anything with anchovies, tuna, garlic, or onions. If you can't tone down the crunchiness of that pickle, the chips, or that hard candy, then leave those noisemakers at home.

Cary Grant did everything short of climbing the walls of the elevator to let a woman exit first. Times have changed. Today, the person closest to the door, man or woman, exits first.

" the only safe topic is the weather "

Quietly excuse yourself if you accidentally push against someone. Keep conversation to a minimum. The only safe topic to discuss in an elevator is the weather.

Discussing claustrophobia or the last time you were stuck in an elevator for ten hours isn't good elevator conversation. Neither is a client's business — that client's brother's doctor's wife's gardener's accountant's hairstylist just may be the annoying gum smacker (also a no-no) standing behind you. You never know who knows whom, so don't take any chances.

Avoid fixing your hair or makeup in the elevator mirror. Dancing to elevator music can be dangerous, too. (Those doors open at the darndest times.) Smoking is forbidden on elevators, and staring should be, as well.

Courtesy also dictates that if you see someone running for the elevator, push the "door open" button rather than the "door close" button. (Otherwise, don't be surprised if that same person — all fired up from nine flights of stairs — is waiting for you on the first floor.)

C all before you send a fax, stating lucidly what you intend to transmit. Send only what is necessary since the paper is supplied on the receiver's end, and you might be tying up the company's telephone line.

Put extra thought into your messages, mindful that others may also have access to them. So, don't send anything confidential unless you're sure your receiver is standing right over the machine.

> " avoid faxes for congratulations or thanks "

Avoid a fax in favor of a written note when relaying a personal message like congratulations, sympathy, or thanks. And don't send your resume via fax unless you really don't want the job.

A cover sheet should ensure that your fax will end up in the right place. Correction fluid may appear as a splotch and colored paper will slow up the transmission; it is better to fax a photocopy.

Make a point of following up your electronic conveyances with a telephone call.

"*If you can't pronounce it, don't order it ...* "
Not necessarily true. However, the only
time to experiment with unfamiliar foods
is on your own time and budget, *not* in a
business situation. If you're in doubt about
how to eat a certain food, use your good
common sense or follow someone else's
lead. If you have a few trouble spots, help
has arrived:

apple: Quarter with a knife. Core and eat with
fingers. Or, cut into smaller pieces and eat with
a fork. If casual, pick up and eat.

asparagus: Finger food unless dripping in
sauce, then use knife and fork.

artichoke: Tear off leaf with fingertips. If
accompanied by lemon butter or vinaigrette, the
part closest to the base is dipped and the leaf
pulled through teeth. Discard the thin inner
leaves and the hairy center. The heart of the
artichoke may be cut and dipped or eaten plain.

avocado: Halved and served in its shell, use
spoon. Sliced on a plate or in a salad, use fork.

bacon: Fingers if crispy, otherwise use fork.

baked potato: Slit with knife and slightly
squeeze with fingers. Add butter and condi-
ments a little at a time. Skin may also be eaten,
cutting as you go.

banana: Peel, cut, and eat with fork at dinner.
Casual setting, peel and eat monkey-style.

barbecued ribs: Definitely finger food.

berries: Spoon.

beverage: Do not use water glass as a finger
bowl. Never dunk anything into your coffee, tea,
or water. Don't blow on a hot drink to cool it or
take water (or ice) and pour some into coffee or
tea. Fruits, olives, or onions in a drink may be
eaten with fingers.

blintzes: Secure with fork and eat with spoon.

bread, rolls, muffins, biscuits: Break off a small piece over the bread plate. Butter the broken portion and eat just that much at a time.

bouillabaisse: (French seafood stew) Use knife and fork to eat fish and lobster. Use spoon to eat the broth.

butter: Place on plate then use to butter bread.

cake (sticky): Fork.

canapés: With a plate, have two, otherwise only one at a time.

cantaloupe, honeydew: Use spoon or fork for balls. Knife and fork for wedge.

caviar: Take a small portion on plate along with toast and garnishes. Spread some caviar on the toast. Top with any or all of the garnishes: chopped egg, onion, or lemon. Eat in bites.

cheese: Spread cheese on a cracker with the accompanying knife. Don't weigh the cracker down. If a wedge, hold with cheese fork and cut off a portion.

cherries: Eaten by hand; pits removed with cupped fingers and placed on dessert plate.

cherry tomatoes: Choose small ones, eat with fingers unless on a salad. Puncturing can be tricky.

chicken wings: Fingers. Place bones on plate.

chips: One at a time. No double dipping or loud crunching.

chocolates: Pick up by paper frill, remove, and eat with fingers.

chops: Secure with a fork and cut into the center or eye of the chop with a sharp knife. If the chop is wearing a frill, hold it by the frill while cutting or pick up the frilled bone and eat from it, if the hostess does.

clams on the half shell: Hold the shell with one, hand and with the seafood fork, remove clam, dip into the sauce and lift to mouth. Only cut a clam, oyster, or mussel if it's fried; then eat with a fork.

cookies: Fingers.

corn on the cob: Butter only two rows at a time and eat.

cornish hen: Disjoint wings and legs with a knife and fork. Remove meat from body and eat with knife and fork. Legs and wings may be eaten with fingers. Follow the hostess's lead.

crab (whole): Remove one leg at a time and crack each into sections with a nutcracker. Remove meat with a seafood fork or a nut pick, dip into sauce or melted butter. Turn crab over and pick out meat with pick or seafood fork.

crab (claws): Pick up with fingers, dip in sauce and suck meat out.

crab (soft shell): Eaten in their entirety — crab and shell — with knife and fork.

crêpes Suzette: Secure with fork and eat with spoon.

crudités: Celery, radishes, olives, pickles, and other veggies are finger foods if used as a garnish or on a relish tray. Do not eat directly from serving tray; put on plate. Pour a little salt or dip on your plate next to the crudité, and dip into it.

cupcakes, brownies: Break in half and eat with fingers.

dips: Dip only once into a community bowl.

egg rolls: Small, use fingers; large, use knife and fork.

fajita: Fill the tortilla with meat and vegetables, add sauces, roll and eat with hands.

figs (fresh): Fingers, if casual. Knife and fork as appetizer. Eat whole fig.

fish (whole): Return it to kitchen to be filleted.

french fries: Fingers, unless large, then cut. Place catsup next to fries and dip into it, don't pour over them.

fried chicken: Fingers, generally. Follow hostess.

frog legs: Cut as much from the bone then, if hostess does, pick up and eat with fingers.

garnish: A lemon slice is a decoration; a wedge is squeezed. Parsley may be picked up and eaten.

grapefruit: Halved and eaten with a teaspoon or a serrated grapefruit spoon.

grapes: Break or cut a cluster then eat with fingers.

gravy, sauce: Spoon onto what it's meant for. Entire entree shouldn't be swimming in gravy. Break off a small piece of bread and place in gravy or sauce and sop it (not slop it) up with fork. This is a compliment to the chef.

ice cream bar: From top to bottom.

jellies: Spoon onto plate next to, not on, meat or fowl. Jelly and meat are then eaten together with fork.

lemon wedge: Puncture first with fork and squirt over shrimp, clams, oysters but not over the sauce.

lobster: Don the lobster bib. Twist off the lobster's big claws with fingers. Use a nutcracker to open the claw, remove the lobster meat with a seafood fork, and dip into the butter. Take the tail meat out in one piece. Cut with a knife and fork, dip into the butter, and eat. The legs are then twisted off with hands and the meat is sucked out — *quietly.* Finally, the tomalley (green liver) of a male lobster or the coral (roe) of the female may be eaten. Go for it!

mango: One way is to cut in half and eat out of the skin, using a spoon. The other way is to cut in quarters, lay it out flat (flesh side down), and pull skin away. Cut. Eat with fork.

mussels (steamed): Lift an *open* shell, separate the mussel from the shell with a seafood fork and dip into the broth and then the melted butter. Eat in one bite. Pile the empty shells on another plate.

mussels (cold): Hold shell, remove mussel with seafood fork, and eat.

olives: Fingers. Remove pit discreetly with cupped fingers.

orange: May be peeled in a continuous spiral with a knife or both ends cut off and cut into vertical sections, peeled and eaten.

oysters (raw on the half shell): Hold by the shell, remove with seafood fork, dip into sauce, and eat in one bite. Never cut.

papaya: Generally served halved with seeds removed. May squirt lime on it. Eat with spoon.

paper wrappers: Open, remove butter, and place the wrapper under the lip of your bread plate.

pasta: Wind a few strands at a time, around a dinner fork, and lift to your mouth. Using a tablespoon and fork is archaic. Do not cut pasta. Hint: ask for a penne or small noodle in a restaurant rather than something messy like spaghetti or linguine.

pâté: Spread on cracker or small toast.

peach: Cut in wedges. Use knife and fork. If casual, pick up and eat.

pie: Fork unless ice cream tops it, then fork and spoon.

pineapple: Knife and fork.

pizza: Hold in fingers with sides slightly up.

potato skins: Fingers. Don't overload.

pound cake: Fingers unless topped with fruit, then fork.

quesadilla: Knife and fork for entree. Fingers for appetizer.

salad: Cut oversized pieces of lettuce with knife. Only use salad fork if salad is a separate course.

sandwich: Knife and fork if large and messy, otherwise pick up and eat with hands.

shrimp (cocktail): Seafood fork. Dip into sauce, and eat.

shrimp (peel and eat): With fingers, remove the shell, hold by tail, dip into sauce, and eat.

shrimp (fried): Served as an entree, use a knife and fork.

shrimp (fantail): Fried Oriental style, pick up by the tail, dip in sauce, and eat.

snails: With snail tongs, grip the hot snail shell and extract the whole snail with a seafood fork. Swallow whole. Broken bread should be dipped into the garlic butter that the snail has been soaking in. Pierce bread with fork, eat and enjoy.

soups: Clear soup, served in small double-handled cups: lift the cup and drink from it. Any vegetables or noodles at the bottom may be eaten with a spoon. Spoon soup away from the table's edge, then bring to mouth. Tilt the bowl away, too. Slurping is o-u-t. Small crackers or croutons may be added a few at a time to the soup.

strawberries: Hold by stem. If cut or in cream, use spoon.

taco: Fingers. Eat from one side only. Don't overstuff.

tangerine: Peel and eat in sections.

toasted ravioli: Fingers as an hors d'oeuvre or fork as entree.

watermelon wedge: Knife and fork. Seeds are removed with cupped fingers.

"**M**iss," a bit old-fashioned, means that a woman has never been married. "Ms." is contemporary, acceptable, and the preferred title for businesswomen.

However, if you know a female colleague prefers "Mrs.," use it rather than offend her. "Mrs." in front of her husband's given name means she is married, whereas "Mrs." in front of her given name means she's divorced. A widow may continue to use her husband's given name if she so desires.

> **only *after* you've received your Ph.D. may you be called Dr.**

If Sally Jones chooses to retain her maiden name when she marries Bill Knight, she is addressed as *"Ms. Jones"* and he as *"Mr. Knight."* The couple would not be addressed as "Mr. and Mrs." Their correspondence is addressed as *"Mr. Bill Knight and Ms. Sally Jones"* all on one line.

When a woman hyphenates her maiden and married names, she is addressed as *"Ms. Mary Jones-Smith."* If Mr. Smith chooses to take his wife's maiden name, Jones, and hyphenate it with his own, the couple may be addressed as *"Mr. and Mrs. William Jones-Smith."* When a woman uses her maiden name only as a middle name, she is referred to socially as "Mrs."

Two married people would be Mr. and Mrs. unless one has a title, in which case they would be addressed as *"The honorable Mary Smith and Mr. Joseph Smith"* on one line, or indent three spaces if you need two lines for a married couple:

*"The Honorable Mary Smith and
    Mr. Joseph Smith"*

When addressing correspondence to two unmarried people living together, it's proper to list their names alphabetically on two separate lines.

*Ms. Mary Kiley
Mr. Joseph Smith*

Address spouse doctors as *"The Doctors Smith,"* or *"Dr. John Smith and Dr. Mary Smith".*

People with Ph.D.s are referred to as "Dr." professionally — socially, only by choice. *"William Smith, Ph.D."* is addressed as such. Socially, he may be called *"Mr. William Smith"* or *"Dr. William Smith".* Only *after* you have received your doctoral degree, may anyone refer to you as Dr.

All correspondence should be addressed with an honorific *or* professional title, but *not* both. An accountant who uses his CPA designation is addressed as *"Donald Cook, CPA"*; a medical doctor as *"Shirley Smith, M.D."* In conversation or when making an introduction, *"Dr. Shirley Smith"* should be used. Socially, Dr. Shirley Smith may be referred to as "Mrs." A married female doctor has this option. A male medical doctor is referred to professionally *and* socially as "Dr."

 If you don't know the title or honorific of the person who will be reading your letter, address it by using the first and last name only. And, if you don't know who will be reading it, address it to *"Dear Reader."*

The title "Esquire," written in full, may be used only in business when addressing an attorney, *"Robert Brown, Esquire."*

A clergyperson should be addressed as "The Reverend" with his or her full name following, such as, *"The Reverend Rosalyn Smith."* Reverend is always preceded by "The" and someone should not be referred to in conversation as Reverend Smith, but rather "Mr.," "Mrs.," "Ms.," or "Dr. Smith" if the clergyperson has a doctoral degree.

"The Honorable" is the preferred courtesy title used in addressing most high-ranking American officials in office or retired. "The Honorable" is not used when speaking to a person or in salutation. Do not use before a surname only. "The" is not capitalized when used in text:

> *"... welcoming address was given by the Honorable William Smith."*

Academic degrees and religious orders should be used in the following order: religious orders, theological degrees, doctoral degrees, honorary degrees. No more than three degrees after a name, *"The Reverend John Mundo, SJ, Ph.D., D.D."*

C hivalry has no place in the office. With all apologies to Sir Lancelot, women and men are treated the same. The little courtesies once shown to a woman in the workplace are no longer expected and, in some situations, are offensive to the female executive.

■ Whoever gets to the door first opens it.

■ When men and women colleagues travel together, meals, taxis, tips, and other expenses are split equally.

■ Whoever hosts a business luncheon pays for it. When a woman is invited to have lunch with her male colleagues, she pays her fair share.

■ A woman should help a man with his coat if he appears to need help.

■ The person closest to the elevator door — man or woman — exits first.

■ It is no longer proper for men to stand when a woman executive enters the meeting room, unless they would stand for a man who holds the same executive position.

■ Men should not expect a woman attending a meeting to get coffee just because she is a woman.

■ We act in the workplace according to protocol, not gender.

giving

Sure, the chia pet you bought as a gag gift for your friend will crack her up. But will your co-worker think "professional" when you surprise him with a ceramic porcupine sprouting green quills? Buying business gifts can be difficult.

Before sending a gift to a client or customer, find out whether it's against company policy.

What to give? A couple of possibilities are items related to a hobby or special interest, donations to a favorite charity, or tickets to an event.

Whatever the reason for giving a gift, think quality! It's much better to give someone a small box of Godiva chocolates than a crate of Yahoo chews. The same applies to a small sterling silver picture frame rather than a large tin one.

Protocol is firm on gifts for the boss — DON'T! However, for a very special occasion, a group gift could be the answer. Speaking of group gifts, companies usually have set policies on employee gift collections; most are discouraged. Refuse politely if you don't want to contribute.

When social and business friendships overlap, it's best to give such gifts outside the office. A few guidelines:

■ Gifts are not a substitute for good business practices.

■ They should never directly follow an order; wait at least three months.

■ Have the gift sent to the home, do not deliver it yourself.

■ Use quality gift wrap.

■ Skip the chia pets.

■ The most appreciated gift says, "I thought about you."

accepting

The well-mannered businessperson accepts gifts with grace and responds quickly with a thank-you note.

declining

The main thing to consider when deciding if it is appropriate to accept a business gift is its appearance to others. Even if you are sure that the gift presented to you is *not a bribe* or a *conflict of interest*, it must pass the "appearance test":

■ Is its value excessive?

■ Was it presented at an unusual time?

■ Would acceptance violate company policy?

■ Might you feel obligated to the person?

■ Does the giver have a reputation for "buying" people?

"
avoid giving gifts to your boss!
"

When your verdict is to decline the gift, it should be returned (within 24 hours) with a handwritten note that thanks the giver but makes it clear that the gift cannot be accepted because of its inappropriateness or company policy.

If you're a recovering alcoholic and someone sends you a case of wine, or you receive a garage door opener and you don't have a garage, keep the gift and let it remain your secret.

W hen in Rome do as the Romans do. But what *do* the Romans do?

When traveling internationally, keep in mind that your way is not the only way of doing things. You might like everyone to speak English or to take a shower (or at least to point you toward the nearest *warm* one), but it won't happen, and you'll have to cope.

Learn some key words, such as "yes," "no," "please," "thank you," "how much," and "where's the toilet," in a foreign tongue. Consider purchasing a tape or a book to teach you such banal buzz words, or ask a college professor to make a language tape for you, or buy a visual translator that allows you to simply point to pictures to communicate.

After you decide where you're going, go to the public library or the U.S. State Department for briefings on the particular country. Get information on the demographics, history, geography, politics, religion, and customs. There are travel books available on numerous countries. (Pick one up when you're purchasing your language translation book.) They include maps, phrases, names of restaurants, transportation information, and much more.

Make copies of your credit cards and the first page of your passport. Don't carry all these items in the same place. Don't give anyone in a foreign country your passport — no matter how big a discount is offered or how big a smile the offerer has. Keep the copy with you at all times.

And remember, when talking to people who aren't English speakers, don't yell. They can hear; they just don't speak your language.

A smile is something everyone understands!

Pay attention to your grooming, or the *powers that be* won't pay much attention to you.

■ Hair should be professionally styled, neatly combed, and clean. Leave the glitz, glitter, and chip-clip out. Hair should not be combed in public and that means your desk.

■ Bushy eyebrows are taboo! If your eyebrows look like pregnant caterpillars, get thee to a pluckery! Tweezers were invented for a reason; use them.

■ Hair growing out of one's nose or ears is repulsive.

■ Forget the beard for business. Men should have a well shaven face and women should shave their legs and under their arms.

■ Women *should* wear makeup. Learn to apply it (cosmetic counters, salons) to enhance your features. A woman does not apply in public — that includes lipstick.

■ Few things betray a woman's status faster than her hands. Fingernails must be polished and all one length. If you bite your nails, do whatever it takes to break this terrible habit. Green, purple, blue, and other obnoxious nail polish colors are unprofessional. Treat yourself to regular manicures.

Polish is not necessary for men, but clean, all one length fingernails are.

Fingernails should be clipped in the privacy of home, not office. No one enjoys listening to the metal tinging of nail clippers in action or dodging the sharp shreds of nail that take to the air.

■ A shower a day keeps the smellies away.

■ Use deodorant.

■ Rinse with a mouthwash after brushing your teeth. Your boss won't be impressed watching you brush in the public rest room.

■ Your favorite scent or aftershave is fine as long as only those close enough to kiss you can smell it.

■ Polish those shoes!

■ Clean and pressed clothing — all of it. (No excuses.)

Don't.

Some people chew gum at the rate of 1,200 rpms or they snap, crack, and pop the offending substance. No one chews gum quietly or looks professional when they do — so don't.

Handshakes range in strength from the wimp to the bone crusher — and yours should be somewhere in between.

The traditional handshake is used in business: Stand. Grasp the other person's palm firmly and hold it for 3 to 4 seconds. Smile. No, you don't grasp a woman's four fingers lightly (unless you want to insult her).

Be eager to shake hands. A handshake is a personal link between you and someone else. It's like dancing: you don't have to say a word to tell the other person exactly what you're thinking.

Shake hands when you meet someone, and again when you leave. In a group, shake hands first with the host.

Don't shake hands if it's obviously impossible. You know the scene — hands full (or up to the wrists in sauce from chomping on chicken wings). When the person has a prosthesis or arthritic hands, place your hand on their forearm or upper arm while saying hello.

Hugging and kissing may be more fun, but the traditional handshake is best for business.

Don't overstay your turn on any of the equipment, especially if someone is waiting for a particular machine.

When you're finished using any of the weight machines or exercise equipment, reset them to the original starting position.

Have a bottle of water to quench your thirst, and a towel to wipe your brow and the equipment if you've soaked it with sweat.

Store your bags and clothing *in* a locker, *on top* of a locker, or *under* a bench; don't strew them all over the locker room.

It's unsanitary to shave in the whirlpools, saunas, or steam showers. For the same reason, most clubs will ask you to shower before entering whirlpools.

If a staff person goes out of his or her way to make your workouts pleasant, drop a note to the management commending this person.

n the hustle and bustle of the holiday season, there's still time for kindness and courtesy. (But then, when isn't there time, right? ... right?)

> "
> ## if in doubt ... send a "Season's Greetings" card
> "

Have you replied to all of your party invitations, you popular little elf, you?

If you're not sure what to wear to a party (that is, just how dressy you should be), call your host and ask. Keep in mind that the holiday season is a time to be a little more flamboyant than other times of the year.

Should someone give you an unexpected holiday gift, don't be embarrassed. Smile and say thanks. People enjoy giving without expecting something in return. (Honestly — some people do!)

If you're in doubt about someone's religious beliefs, it's best to just send "holiday cards" that say, "Season's Greetings," or "Happy Holidays," rather than a card of the completely Christmas or Hanukkah variety.

And, yes, thank-you notes *are* appropriate for holiday gifts and parties. 'Tis the season to be jolly!

When a client, customer, or (ding! ding! ding!) YOUR BOSS (lights flashing! bells ringing!) invites you to his or her home, you've made it into the "big time" corporate world!

Arrive promptly, dressed appropriately with a hostess gift in hand. Watch your alcohol consumption; this is no time to test your tolerance.

Don't lean on the walls (they can stand without your help) or sit on the backs or arms of couches and chairs. That mahogany footrest is really a coffee table, so kindly remove your feet from it.

When offered an alcoholic beverage, refrain from requesting something unusual or exotic. Uh ... just what's in a Hairy Eskimo, Ed? So now two people are embarrassed (especially if neither knows the ingredients).

The gracious host states what he or she is offering rather than, "What do you want to drink?" The answer to this question should be, "What are you serving?"

If the hostess doesn't tell you where to put your glass or offer you a coaster, don't set it down. Never place a glass or dish on an unprotected surface; a water stain isn't the mark you want to leave on your boss.

Don't feel obligated to invite your boss to your home, out to lunch, or to your little brother's Bar Mitzvah. It's something corporate rookies should avoid.

A hostess gift is a way to say thank you to someone who has invited you to his or her home for dinner or a party. It's always a nice gesture to take a small, *quality* gift. Some suggestions are: wine (a nice bottle of, ... none of that kiwi-strawberry stuff), after-dinner liqueur, candy, gourmet salsa, jelly, or something you made. If sending flowers to a hostess, send them the day of the party (and you'll see them) or the day after (to say thank you). Do not bring cut flowers to the hostess.

_____

gift ideas:

- **good wine**

- **liqueur**

- **candy**

- **gourmet salsa**

- **jelly**

- **homemade item**

_____

Don't expect the host or hostess to serve the wine (or whatever else you brought) that evening. Suggest that he or she enjoy this another time.

If you've been asked to sail on someone's yacht (you lucky dog), it is only proper that you take the boat a gift, especially if it's a long sail. Liquor, special food, or a boat accessory of some kind is welcome.

A thank-you note is not necessary when receiving a hostess gift.

Another late night of watching television in a dismal hotel room in a city you thought you'd never visit? Get used to it ...

Hotels range from 5-star to no-star. You will know by this time, what your company guidelines are. Guarantee your reservation with a credit card so when you come wheeling in late some evening, you *will* have a room. On the other hand, if your trip is called off and you don't need a room, cancel the reservation or you will be billed.

If the doorman calls to have your car parked or carries your bags inside to the lobby, tip him. If he just signals for a porter, no tip. Carry your own bags if you can, but don't try to take on ten suitcases just to spare a tip.

Upon arrival, check in at the reservation desk. Request that the reservationist just write down your room number instead of saying it aloud. (Just in case that trench coated person hiding behind the newspaper really *is* up to something.)

Always have the bellman enter the room first so that he gets the brunt of whatever might be waiting for you. That's why you tip him $1 a bag (when he comes to).

You might prefer staying close to an elevator rather than at the end of a very long and quiet corridor. Familiarize yourself with the location of emergency exits, too.

If you are displeased with your room, blow the cobwebs off the telephone and calmly call the front desk to inform the manager of the brown goo globbing from the ceiling or sludging from the faucets, and ask to be moved to another room. Most hotels will accommodate you.

Room service is the boon of a truly nice hotel. Most first-class hotels offer it 24 hours a day. You might find having breakfast in your room an advantage if you have an early morning meeting or appointment. If you choose to have breakfast brought at a certain time, hang the card outside your door before you go to bed. When you're finished with your table or trays, call to have it picked up or leave it in your room, rather than outside your door — a little distasteful to your floor-mates. Usually there is a service charge added to a room service bill; you should tip the server a couple of dollars additional.

Some of the plusher hotels have mini bars stocked with liquor, beer, soft drinks, and snacks. You will be given a key and should feel free to take advantage of this luxury, provided you're willing to *(over)* pay royally for it. There's no charge for the morning paper waiting outside your door.

A hotel will take messages for you. Many of them have voice mail in the room along with another telephone line for your modem or fax machine. Other hotels may have a business service center for your use.

Avoid using your room as a meeting or party room. It's better to ask the concierge to reserve a small meeting space for you, to meet during lunch, or to meet at your client's facility. Meet your clients in the lobby, because turning your room into a party pad decreases your credibility and makes you look immature.

If you signed your bill when you arrived, your charges will be added and you'll find your final bill under your door the morning of checkout. This is express checkout and can be a big help. Leave your key in the room or put it in the key drop box in the lobby.

Most hotels provide an assortment of cosmetics and toiletries in the bathroom, but if you have forgotten something, call housekeeping and it will be delivered to your room. There's no charge, but do tip the delivery person.

The bathrobe, hair dryer, towels, washcloths, extra toilet paper, tissue, ice bucket, glasses, and ash trays aren't for your taking. This is second class and a poor reflection of your company.

Either wear your good jewelry or put it (and any other valuables) in the hotel safe, available at the front desk, but do not leave them in the hotel room.

So the fateful day is approaching ... are your palms sweating just *thinking* about it? With some simple reminders and a little preparation, you will wow your prospective employer.

After cranking out hundreds of resumes, congratulate yourself — now you get to speak with a real person!

Write down the exact time and place of the interview, as well as the name of the interviewer. (Imagine showing up at the wrong time, or getting the name of your interviewer wrong ... you could kiss *that* job good-bye!) Arrive at least 10 to 15 minutes early, showing the interviewer that you're reliable and conscientious.

You should be prepared to talk freely about yourself, highlighting your accomplishments, abilities, and areas of expertise. Show your knowledge of the company; study the annual report; know about the company's prime markets, chief products, key competitors, and plans for future growth. Focus on learning about the position you're vying for and gear most of your answers toward it by highlighting how your skills would enable you to thrive there.

Although you *will* thrive there, don't be overly confident when responding to the interviewer. Greet the interviewer (whether male or female) with a firm handshake, and avoid using first names unless invited to do so. Admit that you've much to learn; and begin your statements with, *"I think,"* or *"From what I know,"* rather than with definite objective phrases such as, *"It's clear that,"* or *"Listen, Ted, everyone knows that ... "*

Be confident, and let this show as you remain relaxed, smiling freely. Positivity is key; beware of statements and actions that may not seem negative to you, but convey such sentiments to the interviewer. (Prepare possible answers ahead of time, and even record them on tape so you can listen for words or tones of voice that may be construed as negative.) Blow your own horn, but don't go overboard with positivity and enthusiasm. (Too much "cotton candy" can make someone sick.)

Be aware of everything; you are being judged from the moment you enter the office (not to add any *more* pressure). Don't just plop down in any chair; wait for the interviewer to offer you one. And beware: there are no innocuous questions. Your answer to every question — from *"How are you?"* (don't rattle off a long-winded answer, even if it *is* positive), to *"Would you like a cup of coffee?"* — is carefully taken into consideration. Decline any food or beverage offers, and never smoke or chew gum.

Pause a moment to think before you answer a question, and answer carefully and non-controversially. (No need to mention how your single-parenting or your leadership in the NRA has readied you. The interviewer might assume you're unfit to travel or spend extra time at the office if you're the only parent raising your children, or that the NRA ... just don't bring it up.) When the interviewer stands, the interview is over.

If an interview takes place over a meal, review Dining Do's and Don'ts. If everyone at the table is having a glass of wine, then have one too, but *only* one glass and no comments on how much (you think) you know about wine.

Afterward, it's a good idea to write a brief synopsis of the interview for your file.

Of course send a thank-you note to your interviewer (or to each interviewer if you had more than one), thanking them for taking the time to meet with you.

Good luck!

When it comes to introductions, you really don't have to be an executive in the Office of Protocol to understand the basics of deference.

Whose name is first? The simple rule is this: you mention *first* the name of the person to whom you're showing deference or honor. A client is shown deference over a staff member or anyone in your company, even your boss.

> *Harry, <u>this is</u> Jane Adams, our new Vice President of Human Resources. Jane, <u>this is</u> Dr. Harry Pratt, President of ABC Company.*

Use the words "<u>this is</u>." Avoid command introductions such as, "Meet so and so."

It's always helpful to provide common ground:

> *You may recall ABC makes those ...*

Most people remember *what you do* rather than *who you are*, but use only professional or official titles, such as <u>Dr</u>., <u>the Honorable</u>, or <u>former President</u> (Ho hum. So many former Presidents ... do the introductions never end?)

yourself: Go up to anyone in any situation and introduce yourself, without an honorific or a title. State your name and something about yourself that establishes common ground.

spouse: If your spouse has the same last name, don't mention it. If it's different from yours, it should be stated (loud and clear). Melissa Jones' husband wouldn't appreciate being called Bill Jones if *his* last name is Smith. Don't use an honorific or title when introducing your spouse.

> *Mr. Old, this is my wife, Bethany Smith-Jones.*

suitemates: Two people living together are introduced with their names. Nothing more needs to be said.

boss: Avoid using the word boss. Instead state his or her position:

> *This is Richard Cool, Manager of our Finance Department.*

secretary: Don't stake claims on a secretary if he or she belongs to the whole department. Remember to say "our" secretary/assistant, not "my" secretary.

If the name wasn't stated clearly, ask to have it repeated and even spelled if you still can't understand it

Acknowledge all introductions with the rhetorical "How do you do?" followed by the person's name. Avoid "I'm pleased to meet you." (How do you know you're pleased to meet this person that you don't even know yet?)

If you have really been looking forward to meeting the person then say so:

I am so glad we finally got to meet. Jeremy has told me a lot about you.

Refer to people the way they are introduced to you. If you've just met someone old enough to be one of your parents, then address that person with an honorific or title (Mr., Mrs., or Dr.) unless they tell you otherwise.

Who stands in an introduction? Everyone. Should the person making the introduction mumble or talk too fast, by all means ask to have it repeated (again and again and again). They will either be pleased to think you want to get the name right or become very annoyed.

If someone misintroduces you, you might smile and respond with:

I'm with ABC Company, not XYZ - or -

Thought you'd like to know my name is Maria not Marie.

Should you misintroduce someone, you might say,

Have you thought about changing your name to ...

It's better to make an incorrect introduction than ignore the person or the situation. Anybody who is somebody won't care if his or her title has been omitted as long as he or she has been introduced.

"**Y**ou are cordially invited ... " "Are you available ... " "Please join us ... "

There are numerous ways to extend business invitations, depending on the occasion: handwritten on your personal stationery, custom-made printed, fill in the blanks invitational cards, and by telephone. Forget faxing or e-mailing an invitation because it's impersonal and unappealing.

When mailing an invitation, do not use labels or a postage meter. The envelope is handwritten in ink, with an honorific or title, and always hand-stamped.

An invitation to your home, should state whether or not there will be smoking. Always invite people "to" dinner at your home, *not* "for" dinner. (You're not carving them up for the main course, you're serving them a meal.)

A response card with an envelope, a map, or any other enclosures, are stacked according to size with the smallest on top.

If you want to receive replies by telephone, use "RSVP" with your telephone number on the lower left-hand side. Avoid "Regrets Only."

A limousine gives class to any occasion. When calling to order a limousine, you might ask the following:

■ What size cars are available? (Limousines range from two-person sedans to six-, eight-, and ten-passenger stretches; consider how many passengers you will have.)

■ What is the charge for the various sizes? Sometimes a stretch costs four times that of a sedan.

■ What colors are available? (This might be important to you; however, accenting the color of your eyes is *not* important.)

■ Can they supply a driver who prefers not to talk? Trying to discuss business with a client while solving your chauffeur's marital problems is tricky.

■ Does the driver know his or her way around town? You want a road concierge.

■ Can you establish an account? If not, which credit cards can be used?

The limo driver is referred to as "driver" or "chauffeur." The driver carries your luggage and opens and closes the door for you.

Tip him or her (preferably cash) between 15 and 20% of the rental charge.

The most comfortable seat in the limo, especially for long legs, is in the front; however, the only difficulty is that person is usually cut off from the conversation in the back. (Which can be a bonus ...) Therefore, the preferred seat is the curbside seat, directly behind the front passenger seat — which means that the junior executive (probably you) gets in the limo first and slides across the seat. Defer to hierarchy.

Listening is a skill that, unfortunately, is untaught.

Who would you rather have for a superior, co-worker, or spouse: someone who talks or someone who listens?

When someone is talking to you, concentrate on what he or she is saying. Visualize and evaluate what you've heard before you speak. Heed the old saying, "Think before you speak."

People like to talk about their successes. Ask questions, and then use and hone your listening skills.

If you cannot repeat what someone is saying to you, then you aren't listening. Salespeople say that they make more sales when they listen to the customer than when they do all of the talking.

Your body language tells whether you're really listening. Look at the person who's talking and keep one thing in mind: everything must come to an end.

A final thought on listening: *No one ever listens himself out of a job!*

Meetings are used for selling, informing, instructing, critiquing, planning, and passing an executive's free time.

attending

Once again, you are new to corporate America and have to pay your dues. Do your homework and go prepared to each meeting.

If the meeting is away from your office, arrive (dressed professionally, of course) a few minutes early and hand your business card to the receptionist or secretary. When shown to the conference room, greet and introduce yourself (with your name, company, and position, if applicable). Don't just plop down anywhere, but look for a table tent with your name on it. If you don't see one on the table, ask, "Where would you like me to sit?" DO NOT sit at the head of the table, unless you're the chairman, then make yourself comfortable there.

The meeting chairman sets the time and tone of the meeting. A courteous chairman may wait ten minutes, but if you're delayed, call to let the chairman know. And don't fall all over yourself with apologies when you arrive. Slip in and be seated.

Have your own note pad and pen ready. Keep your briefcase off the table and the Wrigley's out of your mouth.

If offered something to drink (let's hope it's in a cup or glass, not in a popping bottle or clanging can), it's okay to accept, but don't ask for anything not offered. Use a napkin under your drink. It is *not* the responsibility of the woman in the meeting to get the coffee. No ashtray means no smoking.

Doodling, tapping finger tunes, bending paper clips into tin men, and folding papers into fans show your lack of attention. Tsk, tsk ...

Keep your beeper and cellular phone OFF. Do not ask to use a telephone, unless it pertains to the meeting.

> " **keep your beeper & cellular phone off** "

Be attentive, sit up straight (everything comes to an end). Contribute what you can to the meeting but think before you speak. Avoid arguing. Give credit where credit is due.

If you have to leave early, let the chairman know when you arrive and sit close to the door. A grand exit is not necessary; just leave quietly.

hosting

Should you be hosting a meeting, be selective about the participants and send an agenda. Be sure the room is comfortable and tablets and pencils are on the table. Table tents are nice if it's a large meeting. Put the person's name on both sides. Not because he doesn't know his name, but the person next to him might not know it. Greet outsiders with your coat on. Introduce everyone. Offer refreshments (include cups, glasses and napkins); mints on the table add a nice touch.

A considerate host avoids having meetings first thing Monday morning or late Friday afternoon and tries to end a few minutes early. Most meetings are too long, too dull, too unproductive, and too much a part of corporate life.

The proper placement for a name badge is about four inches down from your *right* shoulder. When shaking hands, the other person's eyes automatically look to your right shoulder. (You can try this experiment at home.)

Spouses who are well known in the company should wear badges with only their names on them. Name badges for unknown spouses should include their names and their spouses' (the employees') names:

> Tom Smith
>
> (Ann Smith)

If the spouse retains her maiden name, Angela Shores, then her name badge would read:

> Angela Shores
>
> (Mrs. Tom Walker)

The only titles that should appear on a name badge are professional titles such as Dr., Judge, or Ambassador, *not* career titles such as president or vice president.

Attendees from different areas and companies may have their company name and location on the badge.

If a woman doesn't want to put her name badge on a suede jacket or silk dress, she would be better off wearing it on her forehead than sticking it on a briefcase. Although it might be painful to remove, she (as well as her name) would be remembered.

national anthem

"Oh say can you see ... " Familiar words that call for Americans to stand, look at the flag, sing if asked to, or keep *perfectly quiet.*

Nothing is so important that it can't wait until the "Star Spangled Banner" or any country's national anthem is over.

During the playing of any national anthem, respect is shown to that country by removing all sport and uniform caps.

A person only salutes or pledges a flag of his or her own country.

Most people network with a purpose. Yours might be to recruit new clients or customers, to get your name out in the community, to change your career (for the better), or to just network. Purpose aside, places to network are corporate sponsored functions, association meetings, seminars, social events, and every time you meet someone new (the list is endless).

> " **break out of your comfort zone ... mingle** "

Whatever professional mission you have in mind, don't forget these crucial strategies for effective networking:

■ Your clothing, behavior and mannerisms will show how confident you are (or aren't) when you enter a room.

■ Forget your own shortcomings and be eager to convert acquaintances into associates and possibly even friends. It doesn't take long if you have the desire.

■ Make direct eye contact (but don't forget to blink).

■ Good posture gives others an impression of competence and self-esteem.

■ If you have an idea of who will be there, develop a list of those people you want to approach. The list can be mental or actual (However, don't walk around the party checking off names.)

■ Smile. Break out of your comfort zone. Mingle.

■ Forget your mother's rule about not talking to strangers (be wary of their candy, though). Go up to anyone and introduce yourself. Waiting for your fairy godmother will get you nowhere. At a company function, state your name and department. At a non-company affair, state your name and your company.

■ Start with an opening question such as, "Where are you from?" and the ball begins rolling.

■ Hanging out at the bar or buffet table waiting for your targets to appear ensures that they won't. It does ensure, however, that Joe Dull will corner you over the cashews and drone your night away with stories about his '89 family reunion at Glacier National Park.

■ If you carry a drink with you, hold it in your left hand, with a cocktail napkin under it. This leaves your right hand free, and you avoid awkward juggling and wet handshakes. Add a plate with food to your right hand and you can forget the handshake all together; just smile.

■ Don't monopolize anyone's time; a few minutes with each person or group of people will keep you mixing and mingling.

■ What a great opportunity to fleece a little free financial advice from your colleague's accountant-wife, right? Wrong. It is unprofessional to question doctors, lawyers, accountants, or any professional to obtain free advice.

■ Have your business cards ready. This may be the opportunity you've been waiting for.

f there's only one piece of advice you take from this book, it is to *pay your dues* when you're the "new kid on the block."

From the minute you first walk in, you should exude friendliness. Be congenial and eager to meet everyone.

Smile (you have a job!); have good eye contact; and offer a firm handshake. You will be sized up and down.

You don't have to be outgoing to be liked. Respond pleasantly to questions and suggestions, and ask for information and assistance courteously. Your teammates will be glad you're on board.

When you're introduced to the people in your department, make sure you get their names right so that you can immediately start calling them by name. That is: by first name if a peer, possibly by last name if a supervisor (remember you refer to people the way they're introduced), and only call your boss by first name when told to do so!

A friendly "good morning" and "good night" on a daily basis to everyone you see can only help. Arrive a few minutes early each day and don't watch the clock to speed out at the stroke of five. (At least finish what you're doing.) If you are working late (a little or a lot), make sure to tell your boss good night when you leave.

Even if you skipped class in college, things are different in the workplace. Rain, snow, or hangover, make every effort to go to work.

In the beginning, while you're still learning your way around, it's difficult to judge your co-workers in a realistic manner. Don't ask personal questions about others in the office. If you form a fast friendship too soon, you may end up in an uncomfortable or restrictive situation.

In a short time, you will know who has power and who doesn't. Beware of being too friendly with the wrong people because you want to be on the right side of the power. It takes some apple polishing, but ostentatious gushing won't do it. Dump the office garbage. Be diplomatic and noncommittal.

Just because you learned one technique in college, or you did something a certain way during your internship at CBA Company ... no one really cares. You may be smart, but you lack experience as a new hiree of ABC Company. Therefore, you must do what ABC wants. This is it! You are here and the real world is a lot different from your college days. To succeed you play the game by the rules or you lose! (Bet you didn't learn that in school.)

Being the gopher (go fer this and go fer that) will quickly show you that you're the low man on the totem pole. Once you promise to get something to or for someone, keep your promise. This is the way to gain credibility. Don't take the pens, pencils, telephone message pads, or any other supplies home.

Whenever you are given a project, go out of your way to do a good job. Give it at least 110% of your time and ability. Your enthusiasm, or lack thereof, will be visible. If you make a mistake, admit it, apologize, and do your best to correct it.

Don't pass the buck when you can do something to help someone. "That's not my job," or "I don't really care," are attitudes that will keep you from advancing.

When someone stops in your office to talk to you about something, stop what you're doing and give him or her your undivided attention. If you're running against a time restraint, explain it and ask if you can get back to that person.

Backslapping, touching, winking, and flirting will only limit your chances to climb. Keep your hands to yourself. That means no snooping on anyone's desk or prying for information, either.

Your boss hired you. There is obviously something he or she likes about you. (I know — in addition to your 3.9 GPA, you have *class*.) Be loyal to your boss. Loyalty has its rewards.

Don't try to outshine, humiliate or correct your boss in front of others — he or she is the boss and, sad as it may seem, determines your future at ABC Company. Show your boss the deference he or she is due. You'll know someday what it's like.

Place cards are a great way to seat your guests at a dinner party, at home, or at your club.

It's proper to have just a person's title, or honorific, and last name on the place card, such as:

Dr. Smith

Ms. Jones

Should two people have the same last name, include their first names. Or, if no one knows anyone else, use first and last names:

Ms. Mary Smith

Ms. Jennifer Smith

Elected officials (current and former) or people of rank must have either their rank or "The Honorable" preceding their names:

The Honorable Thomas F. Kiley

What if you don't like the person you're sitting next to or you feel you should have a better seat? You're out of luck; place cards stay where they are put and so should you.

When invited to a private club, be it athletic, country, dinner, or professional, you are someone's guest. Your misbehavior could be a source of embarrassment for your host.

If you are even the least bit doubtful, ask your host what the dress code is. When coat and tie are appropriate dinner attire, showing up without them (or the feminine equivalent) won't win points with your boss.

A guest does not pay or tip at a private club; there is no exchange of money. The member simply signs a form called a chit, and is billed for the service. The club assesses members a gratuity for service personnel.

A corporate party consisting of 60 or more guests should have a receiving line.

If there is a greeter, he or she will introduce you to the first person, who will introduce you to the next person, and so on until you've been introduced to the first few people. Then, you're on your own, so extend your hand (no drinks) and state clearly your name and company to each person.

This is not the time to air your views, political or otherwise; so smile, shake hands, and keep right on moving.

When you are being recruited by a company or maybe companies, remember to:

Read this book from beginning to end.

Mind your manners.

Exude confidence.

Don't try to remember everyone's name at a social business (isn't that an oxymoron?) function. Be selective.

When being introduced, forget your own shortcomings or anything else on your mind. Concentrate on the introduction.

Repeat the name when you acknowledge the introduction so that you've heard it twice. If the name is unclear, ask to have it repeated or even spelled. (After four times, people may become irritated to think you can't get their names straight, or they may be honored to think you really want to say them correctly. Either way, make sure you've got their names.)

Now, open a mental file. (That's right, *in your mind ...*) In it place that person's name and anything else you can remember or can associate with the name: a distinctive characteristic like a striking (or *not* so striking) facial feature, manner of dress, hairstyle, eyeglasses' shape, stature, or even something the person has said to you.

Using association, here are a few ways to help you remember names:

■ Think of another person you know or have known with the same first name.

■ Come up with symbols pertaining to the person's name. For example, Joan Green. Green can be associated with money or grass. (Let your imagination take it from there ...)

■ For a difficult name, say it several times to yourself, breaking it into syllables. Perniciaro. Per Knee Share O.

■ If the name is easy to forget, think of a rhyming action. Dave is waving or shaving. Sandy's handy or eating candy.

Then, when you go home, write down all of the salient facts you can remember about that person on an index card. Make these cards up each time you meet someone and you'll have a file. You may even go so far as to categorize your file by "single men/women," (a good file to keep handy, huh?) or "potential clients."

The mind is wonderful; it begins working the minute we're born and doesn't stop until we have to remember someone's name.

In any situation, avoid surprising someone with, *"Do you remember me?"* When you hear the answer, you might be sorry you asked. Instead, reintroduce yourself and admit you've forgotten the person's name. It happens to everyone.

If you can pull it off, here are a few phrases you might use: *"Do you happen to remember your name?" "Yesterday I forgot my mother's name, today I've forgotten yours,"* or *"It's genetic in my family; after 21 we forget names."*

To use the stale phrase, *"I'm terrible at remembering names,"* is OK, but it's the easy way out. You have to have the desire to remember names (you can practice all you want, but if you don't have the desire ...). It takes work and practice, too, but it's well worth the effort because you'll be remembered as a person who cares. (Isn't that how we'd all like to be remembered?)

A s you climb your way up the corporate ladder, you may become responsible for hosting business meals.

The whole idea of a business meal seems to violate the cliché, "Don't mix business with pleasure." However, effective business meals are just that: *business meetings over meals ...* and should be treated as such.

If you only have an hour, meet for breakfast; two hours, have lunch; and if you have all evening, go to dinner. However, if this is your first invitation to someone, it should be for breakfast or lunch, not dinner.

The first invitation comes directly from the host, not a secretary or assistant. When asking someone to breakfast or lunch, mention the reason and be specific about the date. *"Sandra let's discuss ABC over lunch. Are you available next Wednesday?"*

Unless you offer two places and allow your guest to choose one, it is your responsibility as host to choose the restaurant. You might ask, *"There's a wonderful Italian restaurant, a new Chinese restaurant, or do you prefer steak?"* Rather than asking, *"Where do you want to eat?"*

With the exception of breakfast, it's a good idea to make a reservation. It's not a good idea to make four reservations at four different restaurants and ignore three of them. If you can't get a reservation, try someplace else. (Never use a prominent person's name or pretend to be someone you aren't.)

When making your reservation, it's okay to request a certain table and ask about the dress code if you're unfamiliar with it. It's also perfectly proper to meet the maître d' the day before a very important dinner, to introduce yourself and choose the table you want (away from the kitchen, the rest rooms, or a mirror). He, of course gets tipped (in cash) on your way out the door on the big evening.

Should plans change, call to cancel your reservation.

On the day of your meeting, confirm your reservation with the restaurant and also with your guest(s). Tell your guest (especially if he or she is from out of town) what kind of restaurant it is, if you're eating outside in a cabana, and if there is a dress code.

If you plan to meet at the restaurant, arrive early. You may wait in the lobby, go to the cocktail lounge, or be seated at the table. Make sure the maître d' knows where to find you. Should you be delayed, call the restaurant to let them and your guest(s) know.

Coats are less cumbersome if checked. Should a woman choose to keep hers, she is seated and her coat is removed from her shoulders and placed onto the back of her chair. No one takes an extra chair for coats or accessories. Briefcases and handbags are on the floor or on your lap, never on the table. A man removes a hat indoors.

As the host, you may order a drink while waiting, but avoid eating the crackers or bread sticks. A guest does not order anything to drink while waiting for the host. If you're in the cocktail lounge and called to be seated, the waiter carries your drink to the table. Some restaurants will give you a vibrating beeper to let you know when your table is ready.

When you are the host, decide beforehand just where you want your guests to sit. You should choose the most advantageous position for yourself.

Once seated, offer your guest a drink (with the exception of breakfast). If he or she declines, so should you. If he or she chooses to have a drink, and you don't want alcohol, you should order something from the bar anyway (like orange juice or a club soda with lime).

It's OK to suggest a couple of the more expensive items, such as, *"I'm having the lobster newburg; it's excellent and definitely something I would suggest if you like seafood. Although I've never had it, the steak Diane is supposed to be outstanding."*

Choose the same number of courses as your guest (even if you can't eat it all) and pace your eating speed with that of your guest.

If food is prepared improperly or if you discover a foreign object in it (alive or otherwise), the host — *not* the guest — should summon the waiter and send it back. If it's something new you're trying and you don't happen to like the taste of it ... too bad. Business meals are not the time to experiment.

A dropped utensil stays on the floor and the waiter is asked to get another one.

Your napkin is placed on the table, not the chair, if you have to get up during a meal.

Keep the noise down. Avoid table hopping or joining in a conversation at the next table. A woman does not groom herself or reapply her lipstick at the table. If you must get up during a meal, place your napkin on the table, *not* your chair.

As the host, signal that the meal is over by requesting the check (which is always placed face down) or crumple your napkin and put it on the table. A classy touch is not to have the check brought to the table, but to give the waiter your credit card and ask to have the receipt mailed to your office. If you frequent a restaurant, you might even establish an account and then the charges will be mailed directly to you.

breakfast

The best place to go for breakfast is the dining room or the coffee shop of a major hotel. Some people just drink coffee and call it breakfast. If your guest orders more than a bagel, so should you.

lunch

The first 10 to15 minutes at breakfast and lunch should be small talk. After you've given your order, say something like, *"Well, let's get down to why we're here ..."* Or, *"As you know, I wanted to discuss ABC with you ..."*

dinner

Different parts of the country (and world) maintain different eating hours. If your guest is from out of town, ask what time he or she likes to dine and if he or she has any food preferences. Asking these questions in advance will be helpful in choosing a restaurant.

Since dinner is the most social of the three meals, it's nice to include a spouse. If the spouse plans to attend, make it a foursome to make conversation easier. Otherwise, discussing business may create an awkward situation.

Offer a drink before the meal, then have casual conversation for about 30 minutes. Order dinner. Offer wine with dinner. If the wine steward fails to return after pouring the first glass of wine, the host or hostess may remove the bottle from the wine bucket and refill the glasses, beginning with the guest's.

Discuss business but keep the conversation fairly social. Always offer coffee and dessert, and possibly an after dinner drink.

Restaurant dining should be a pleasurable experi-ence; however, if you are dissatisfied, the manage-ment of any good restaurant wants to know, so call or write a letter. It isn't your responsibility to reprimand the waitstaff.

A couple of terms explained:

à la carte (ah lah KART): each part of a meal or dish (salad, vegetable) is priced separately, and is consequently more expensive

prix fixe (pree FEEX): fixed price for a meal with several courses.

maitre d' or headwaiter: Stands at the entrance to the dining room. He shows you to your table and seats you. He is the man to talk to about any special service you desire and generally can be easily identified by his tuxedo. He may also act as the captain (see below) in a smaller restaurant.

captain: Also may wear a tuxedo, takes your order and sees that it is prepared correctly and served properly.

waiter/waitress: Picks up your order from the kitchen, bar, or dessert area and serves it to you.

busboys: Responsible for cleaning your table, filling your water glasses, and providing clean ashtrays.

wine steward: Presents the wine list to the host, who may ask him to suggest an appropriate wine.

How do you address the staff? By the way they introduce themselves to you. Avoid "miss," "honey," "busboy," or "boy." (Could you be any *more* condescending?) People like to be shown respect, so favor "sir" and "ma'am" over "waiter" and "waitress." The '90s way (the politically correct way) to refer to a waiter or waitress is to call him or her "waitperson."

wrong	right
waiter	sir
miss	ma'am
honey	
busboy	
boy	

It isn't necessary to carry on a conversation with the waiter (oops! waitperson). On the other hand, some people clam up as soon as the waitstaff appears for fear they'll hear what's being said. To quote Rosina Harrison, Lady Astor's personal maid for many years, "It's difficult if you start getting interested in what's being said among the guests because if you do, your concentration goes." In other words, no one has time to listen.

How many times should you say, "thank you" to those waiting on you? Every time they show you a courtesy.

We've all seen them, but what do they mean? Those esoteric four letters at the bottom of an invitation — RSVP — tend to bewilder some people. (Which is probably why they ignore them.)

RSVP, an abbreviation of a French phrase, has seeped into American society. It stands for "répondez s'il vous plait," which (in a very rough translation) means, "Are you coming or not?" RSVP is commonly confused with "Regrets only," which should be avoided all together.

What is the most appropriate way to RSVP? If time allows, respond by note, courteously accepting or declining the invitation in writing. However, most invitations today will include a telephone number, so use it. The classy way to telephone a response is not to say, *"I'm calling to r-s-v-p"* but rather, *"I am calling to accept your invitation to dinner next week,"* or, *"I'm replying to your ... "*

Whichever way you respond, it is crucial that you do so as soon after receiving the invitation as possible (within 24 hours). Not even the most gracious host appreciates guests who phone 15 minutes before the event begins, or worse yet those who do not acknowledge the invitation at all and show up! Once you have accepted an invitation you are bound ... even if something better comes along.

Unavailable? Decline the invitation rather than send someone in your place.

If you're the host and no one responds to your invitation, you have two choices: call everyone you've invited or turn off the lights and go out.

Remember Sally Fresner's birthday parties with all of the party hats, candy, and games? The days of blindly mounting masking-taped tails on a mule are long gone. They have given way to the corporate party, or "partying with a purpose."

In the workplace we call those occasions where your presence *is* expected *command performances*. They include, but are not limited to, the company picnic, the holiday party, client cocktail parties, company-sponsored fund raisers, the hospitality suite, honorary dinners, organized sporting and cultural events, and most importantly, invitations from your boss (gulp!). A major corporate function can provide the perfect opportunity to ruin your career — which is why most employees prefer to stay home. A brief description of these swanky and not so swanky affairs follows:

cocktail party: drinks and hors d'oeuvres; lasts 1-1/2 to 2 hours between 5 and 8 p.m.; guests stand; business attire.

cocktail buffet: drinks and dinner foods; lasts 2 to 3 hours between 6 and 9 p.m.; guests serve themselves and randomly sit at tables; business attire.

reception: elaborate hors d'oeuvres served by waiters; is held before dinner between 6 and 8 p.m.; generally a receiving line; protocol conscious, it's usually honoring someone; business attire, but dressier for women.

brunch: combination of breakfast and lunch between 11 a.m. and 2 p.m.; may be sit down or a buffet; table assignments; business casual/ business attire.

picnic: outdoors; casual foods (burgers, ribs, barbecue); paper and plastic utensils; casual attire.

tailgate: before a sporting event or outdoor concert; can be simple or elegant with a car trunk being the table; casual attire.

beach/pool party: casual attire; if wearing a swimsuit, have an appropriate cover up and change of clothing.

When you reply to the invitation, find out as much about the guest list as possible. Knowing who will be there will make networking easier.

It's not cute to show up wearing a tee shirt with a coat or shorts with a tie. A woman should not wear a dress that's too tight, too short, or too revealing. Dressing appropriately is a must.

Show up. (Period.) Arrive no later than 15 minutes after the designated time.

Mingle with higher ups, the very people you have limited contact with.

Ignoring the boss, president, chairman, or their spouses, may be noticed and looked upon unfavorably. It's like being invited to a party and snubbing the guest of honor; don't expect an invitation next year (and you can forget seconds on dessert as well).

Being the boss's best buddy and insisting on discussing business is a faux pas (that means bungling it up).

Many senior members of management actually feel socially inept (because they weren't as lucky as you to have had a book *specifically written* for *them* when *they* first entered the job market ...), so don't be intimidated.

No one has a perfect boss, so don't gossip about yours.

This is not the time to ask your boss for a favor, monopolize a celebrity or VIP, or ask any professional for free advice. *("Say, Doc, could you just look at my ... ")*

Don't sic your spouse on your boss for a favor. *("Beth, I know I can talk with you 'woman to woman;' we both know that Tom really deserves a raise ... ")*

Leave loud, obnoxious behavior and insulting humor at home.

Avoid flirting and making advances.

Don't fill up your plate at an hors d'oeuvre table as if it's your last meal. This evidences glutton-ous, low class moochery. It's better to go back for seconds.

When being served hors d'oeuvres or canapés, you may take two if you have a plate, otherwise just take one at a time.

Don't stick a toothpick in a piece of food and put it directly in your mouth. Put it on your plate, then eat it. What to do with the toothpick or the drink stirrer (no it isn't a straw) when you're finished? Place it on the server's tray or hold it with your napkin until you can dispose of it properly. Do not put it on the buffet table.

While eating, hold the cocktail napkin under your plate; while drinking, it stays in your left hand, under your glass.

Keep your drink in your left hand to free your right hand for shaking hands. Add a plate of food and just smile instead of shaking, unless you can balance the plate on your head.

Do not eat, drink, and talk all at the same time; doing any two at a time won't work either.

Over drinking is not cool. Know your limit and don't strive to reach it.

Partake in any of the planned activities. They are someone's (don't question whose) idea of fun, so don't be a dud.

Mother Nature is not in charge of the environment — we are, so please don't litter.

A towel on a lounge chair means that the chair is taken, so don't take the towel *or* the chair.

Not everyone plans to get in the water or even get wet at a pool party, so please be respectful.

Leave at, or shortly before, the time designated on your invitation.

Making a great impression doesn't depend on making a grand exit. Your host or hostess will likely be busy entertaining guests. Don't interrupt, but certainly send a thank-you note the next day.

Even if you don't get out much, act as if you do.

You've probably heard all this before ... from your mother (What a smart woman!).

As the corporate host, decide beforehand just where you want your guests to sit. You should choose the most advantageous position for yourself and say, *"Mary, why don't you sit here and Bill, you sit next to Dave."*

If you are the guest, ask where the host would like you to sit. Should it make no difference to the host, sit in the chair closest to you.

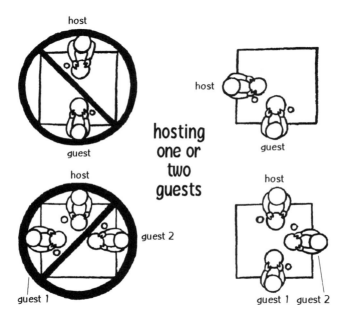

hosting one or two guests

hosting multiples of four with a spouse

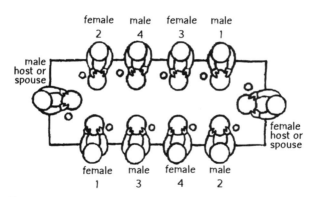

Seminars and association meetings are for companies or industries with a focus on information, development, and problem solving.

New products and ideas are introduced, people are honored (or dishonored), and careers are made. Make seminars work for you!

> " seminars can be ideal for networking & career advancement "

If you're lucky enough to be asked to make a presentation, take advantage of an opportunity to do a great job. Do some planning, put some *extra* time into it. All eyes will be on you, so set the groundwork for your path to the CEO chair.

Network. Social business situations are the time to shine not whine. Go up to anyone, introduce yourself (conveniently located elsewhere in this handy book), and begin a conversation ... who knows what might come from it?

An absent ashtray means "No smoking," so don't even think about asking for one. Abide by all laws governing smoking.

Never force your non-smoking guest to sit in a smoking section, even if you prefer to smoke. If you don't smoke and your guest does, accommodate your guest if you can.

If ashtrays are on the table, avoid smoking during a meal and in-between courses. The only time to smoke is after dessert, *if* smoking is permitted.

When extending an invitation, you have an obligation to tell your guests that your home is smoke-free, or that smoking is permitted on the patio, or around the corner, three blocks away.

don't smoke in:

- a car
- an elevator
- non-smoking areas
- your host's bathroom
- where there are no ashtrays

If your host offers you an ashtray, rinse it when you're finished. Be sensitive to where your smoke is drifting and switch directions if necessary. Smoking in someone's bathroom is tacky; the smoke stench lingers, anyway. If you have to smoke, go outside with an ashtray; don't throw your butts all over the patio. Don't light up in a car full of people and never smoke on an elevator.

spectator

Be familiar with the rules of the game and even do some research on the players so that you have a vague idea of who's who, what they're doing, and why.

Avoid quoting facts unless you're absolutely sure you know what you're talking about. (And even then, don't be belligerent.)

Dress casually and avoid jeans in a business situation. Arrive on time or, better yet, before the game starts.

It's OK to yell and cheer, but don't spout off everything that's on your mind. (Keep the obscenities to yourself.) When you jump up, remember to sit back down quickly.

If you get up during the game, return to your seat only when there's a break in the action. Wait at the top of the stairs so that you don't disturb the other spectators.

As someone's guest, root for the host's team — especially if you're with the boss. Be sympathetic if your boss's team is unmercifully defeated, (even if you *are* delighted).

Watch your food consumption, but more importantly, watch your alcohol consumption. Offer to buy a drink and something to eat for your host and the other people in your party.

" **congratulate the winners ... compliment the losers** "

It's a fun opportunity if you're invited to watch a sporting event from a private box. Generally used by companies for entertaining purposes, they are enclosed and exclusive of the regular seats. There may be a dress code; attire can be anything from black tie to casual. Ask, if you're unsure of how to dress. Food and drink are provided, and sometimes may be ordered from a special menu.

participant

Clubs usually have dress codes for various sports. Find out what the dress code is and abide by it, including the right shoes.

Don't cancel. If something prevents you from playing, offer to find someone to fill in but don't automatically send someone else.

Arrive early to allow time for warming up. You wouldn't want to make everyone in your party miss a tee time, now would you?

Have your own equipment — balls, racquet, clubs.

Be honest about your ability. Don't pour it on when you are better than someone, but don't patronize your opponent by slacking off, either.

Don't complain or whine about your playing (or anyone else's, especially your partner's). It's not necessary to comment, critique, or give unsolicited advice to your partner or opponent. Avoid cursing or throwing your racquet or clubs.

Don't have just a vague idea of the rules — *know* them, *live* them.

At all times, keep your voice down and when necessary be silent and still (when someone's teeing off). When in doubt, zip it up.

Holding up the game to tell jokes, stopping for a drink, or taking a telephone call (heaven forbid) is rude.

Avoid challenging anyone's call or score, even if you know it's wrong. Worse yet is *cheating* ... don't.

Congratulate the winners, compliment the losers. Tell everyone how much you enjoyed yourself.

Sportsmanship, like courage, is "grace" under pressure.

Pay your bets (this is part of being a good sport) and head to the 19th hole. Play it right, and you'll score high in your career.

Many companies include spouses at annual meetings when at spas or resorts.

If planning "Spouse Activities," do so with care because the days of making lace doilies in "little women programs" are over.

A good speaker is always a plus; exercise classes and sports tournaments are usually successful. Male spouses may be excused from the activity if they are awkwardly in the minority.

The important thing here is for the spouse to be allowed to participate in as many meetings as possible with his or her mate, especially if the guest speaker has an interesting message. (Doilies are *not* interesting.) This also allows the spouse to have a better understanding of the company's business. (Unless the company is the leading doily manufacturer.)

As for apartment mates, lovers, or dates who may join single professionals, they too have responsibilities to act discreetly and participate along with everyone else. If the president or chairman of the board and his or her spouse disapprove of significant others, it's best to get single rooms.

A spouse who remains aloof from the rest of the crowd is not doing his or her mate any good at all. Some sound advice for the spouse who is easily bored or usually unenthusiastic: Stay home!

S urely by now you've made at least a
dozen speeches, but did you enjoy them?
Public speaking is a dreaded fear — and
why? You, too, can talk.

Practice, drill, and rehearse. Know your
material. Strive for excellence, *not*
perfection. Know your material. Don't try to
get rid of your butterflies, just put them in
order. Know your material.

The night before
you give your
speech, read it
over before you
go to bed, and
then get a good
night's sleep.

Take all the *stuff*
(eyeglasses,
wadded up
handkerchief,
grocery list, car
keys, taxi receipts,
notepad from
hotel) out of your
pockets.

Walk up to the
podium with good
posture, exuding the confidence you've
gained from knowing your material so well.
Imagine everyone sitting there naked? How
nauseating. Choose one person. Look at
that person and smile. She will be a nervous
wreck thinking you're going to call on her. If
you're using notes, keep them away from

your face, and use them as reminders —
don't just read from them.

The podium will
stand up alone,
so you don't
have to hold it
up. If you lean
on it too much,
it might fall over.

Unless you're a
professional
comedian, don't
try to be the life
of the podium.
Your humor will go over like a lead balloon.

Three rules:

1. know your material

2. know your material

3. know your material

————————,,

Picture this — you're in the middle of your
speech and your mind goes blank —
completely blank (avoid stammering
"uh ... uh ... uh ... uh ... " — this is a dead
giveaway). Instead, stop, look at your
audience, and smile. Your audience will be
on the edges of their seats. They won't
have a clue whether you've forgotten your
next line or you're going to make some
earth-shattering statement. If nothing
comes back to you, smile and end it. (90%
of the people probably aren't paying any
attention to what you're saying, anyway.)

On the other side of the podium, the
nicest gift you can give a speaker is
your attention.

Business letterhead is 8-1/2 x 11" and is used just for business.

Choose a high-quality paper for your personal stationery. Papers made from 100% cotton fiber (no, not a napkin!) are best.

A stationery wardrobe can consist of any number of different papers. Just two are really necessary — one for letters and one for notes. A monarch sheet measuring 7-1/2 x 10-1/2" may be used for letters. When you reach a certain rung of the corporate ladder, you may be entitled to monarch or personal business stationery. This letterhead will have your name, career title, and company address. You will use this for personal business notes.

An informal is a small fold-over note card (begin writing under the fold) used for gift enclosures, thank-you notes, to respond to invitations, as well as to send brief messages. Some companies have their corporate logo on the front of their informals.

One of the most useful items in a stationery wardrobe is a correspondence card, which is a flat, heavy card mailed in a matching envelope. These cards are used for thank-yous, informal invitations, and short notes. Write on the back if you need more room.

Because letters and notes are written by only one person, only one person's name or monogram properly appears on the stationery. On social stationery, the return address (address only, no name) is on the back of the envelope. In business, the company name and address are in the upper left hand corner.

Envelopes should match your stationery. It is really tacky to scratch out "Jubilee Inn" and put your name or return sticker on it.

Your personal stationery makes a statement about you. Save the lime green and hot pink for those times when you don't want to be taken seriously.

The properly set table

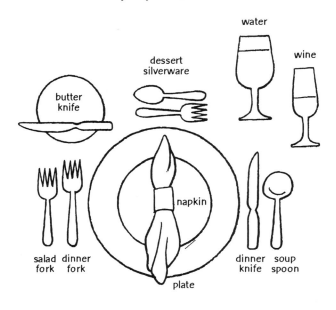

water

wine

dessert
silverware

butter
knife

napkin

salad   dinner
fork   fork

dinner soup
knife   spoon

plate

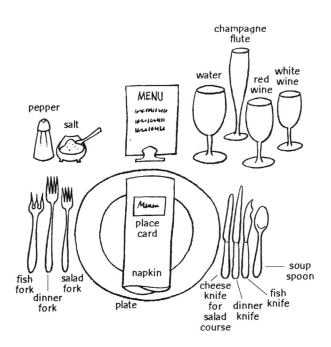

champagne
flute

water

red   white
wine   wine

pepper

salt

MENU

place
card

napkin

fish   salad
fork   fork

dinner
fork

plate

cheese
knife
for
salad
course

dinner
knife

fish
knife

soup
spoon

The corporate host or person of lesser rank has the honor of hailing a cab. Take the next cab in line when at a cab stand; it's not a game of pick and choose.

The preferred seat in a cab or limousine is the rear passenger side, which is where you sit if traveling alone. Otherwise, hierarchy ... and the client or customer ranks higher than anyone in your organization.

Some cab drivers will take a credit card, but all take cash. Tip 15 to 20% of the cost. Be sure to get a receipt.

Not long ago only debutantes and blue-haired ladies took tea in the afternoon. Now businesspeople are making deals over tea; lovers are making plans over tea; and many are making mistakes over tea ...

The atmosphere is distinguished and relaxed. Check with the most elegant hotels to see if and when they serve tea. Expect to be seated between 2 and 5 p.m.. Plan to stay for a couple of hours. Dress is chic business attire.

Tea is served in a series of courses. The first is the tea itself. You will have a choice of teas, so expand your caffeinated horizons.

If the tea is loose, it will be served in a little silver strainer and must steep three to five minutes before being imbibed. Some tea rooms will offer a variety of tea bags, and often your waiter or waitress will pour the tea.

Flavor your tea with sugar, lemon, or milk. (*Cream* is for coffee!) You can mimic the Queen of England, a *real* tea drinker, and put your milk in first.

The second course is a scrumptious assortment of finger sandwiches, appropriately named because they are eaten with your fingers. They are filled with pâté, watercress, salmon, cucumber, or Spam. (Yeah, right!)

The sweets come next. Use your fork for the messy pastries, otherwise use your fingers, keeping in mind that *nothing* is finger lickin' good.

Toward the meal's end, you may wish to order a glass of dry sherry to prepare you for the **check**, which will be worth every penny.

This is known as "afternoon tea," which is quite different from the "high tea" meal of meat and potatoes served to England's blue collar workers who ate in the scullery, standing at a "high" table. If you refer to afternoon tea as "high" tea, you deserve not to be there.

W hen used properly, the telephone can serve as a company's most valuable tool!

answering

A telephone should be answered before the third ring. To the caller, the person answering the telephone *is* the company, conveying its spirit, enthusiasm, and professionalism (or lack thereof). The phone should be answered with a friendly greeting and the company name (clearly stated). A smile when answering the telephone is transmitted to the person calling. (You can *hear* facial expressions.)

screening

It's difficult to properly screen a call. *"Who's calling?"* automatically puts the caller on the defensive. It's better to say something such as, *"I'm speaking with?"* or, *"And you are?"*

If someone seems hesitant about giving his or her name, you might tell the caller that Ms. Rodgers likes to know who is calling.

Don't ask, *"May I help you?"* or *"to what does this pertain?"* Instead it's better to offer help by saying, *"How may I help you?"*

Forget the slang: *"She's tied up"* sounds like bondage, and *"hang on"* dangles the caller from the edge of a cliff.

hold button

The hold button is an unavoidable evil. It's frustrating to be put on hold and then kept waiting and waiting and waiting. Before putting people on hold, tell them why you must do so. *"I'm sorry, Mr. Smith, but I have to locate Ms. Jones."* Or, *"I have another telephone ringing, are you able to hold just a moment?"* If the caller cannot wait, take his or her number and have the call returned.

Keep the golden rule in mind when your finger is hovering above the heinous hold button; no one likes to be (or should be) kept on hold for longer than *ten seconds.*

call waiting

Call waiting is handled just like the hold button. Always go back to the first caller. The second caller has the choice of waiting or hanging up.

transferring

When you have to transfer a call to another department, be sure to tell the caller why, where, and to whom. *"I'm going to transfer you to the accounting department, where Jim Brown, the accounts payable manager, will be able to help you. He is at extension 1234."* Then, if you really want to give a wonderful impression of your company, you'll call the person later in the day to see if Jim Brown solved the problem. (Of course, you may be opening a can of worms, so be ready to offer another alternative to the caller if Jim Brown failed to solve anything.)

answering your telephone

When answering your own telephone, speak clearly and slowly. Answer with your *first and last name.* A department can't answer the telephone, but a real live person can, and that's who the caller wants. Don't use "Yo" or any other grunting sound as a greeting either.

placing a call

When making a call, identify yourself and your company each time (so the person answering doesn't have to screen the call). You may not get through to the person you're seeking, but it still shows you have integrity. After several attempts, you might ask the secretary how you go about making a telephone appointment. By the way, don't bypass a secretary. Secretaries have a direct connection to their managers' daily schedules and therefore wield a great deal of power. Befriending secretaries is a wise move.

speaker phone

When you put people on speaker phones, tell them right away and inform them of the presence of others — who should then greet the person on the phone.

returning calls

Each person should return his or her calls daily. Unless a party requests that you call him or her at home, *do not*. Home time is personal time.

wrong number

If you reach a wrong number, apologize rather than just hang up.

public phone

Keep your distance instead of eavesdropping. Avoid staring or looking at your watch. If you're the one making a call, be quick because other people may want to use the phone.

miscellaneous

No gumdrops, please. Sipping, lip smacking, and ice crunching are annoying and should be avoided.

Forget the three-way conversations. Talk with only the person on the other end of the line.

Hold the mouthpiece about one inch from your mouth, not on your shoulder while you're doing something else.

It's better to sign off by saying "*good-bye*" rather than *"ciao," "catch ya on the flip side,"* or *"bye bye."*

When is a thank-you note appropriate? When someone does something for you, gives you something, or invites you to be his or her guest. When in doubt, err on the side of graciousness — send it. A telephone or oral thank-you is not enough when you consider that someone has gone out of his or her way to do something for you. (Really, it's the *least* you can do!)

Send a thank-you note within 24 hours of whatever you received (got it?). This way your real feelings will creep into it (this is usually good). Timeliness is impressive.

Even if you forget to send the note and three months have elapsed and you've lost and/or broken the favored fly swatter and its grantor has moved to Geneva ... still write it and tell the person "how much you've enjoyed using the ... " They will know you forgot, but write it anyway.

OK, you've made the big decision to send a note. Now, what should you say? Thank the person for his or her gift. Mention what you like about it. Write what you're going to do with it or how much you've been wanting one. By the way, use the phrase "thank you very much" only once in a note.

Can't find one thing you like about the gift? Thank the person for his or her thoughtfulness. Avoid ever asking a favor in a thank you note.

Personalize a canned note (in business, the same note may be typed to everyone) by handwriting a note on the bottom. Business is the only time you may type a thank-you note. Otherwise, they should be handwritten, legibly, in ink.

If more than one person gave you a gift, send a note to only one person, but mention the others.

An inappropriate gift is returned with a "thank-you-but-no-thank-you" note.

If you use an informal note, begin writing under the fold. You may also use a correspondence card; however, avoid writing a thank-you note for a monetary gift (such as your bonus) on the back of a check. This is tacky.

Have you ever spent a theatrical performance cursing the candy cruncher sitting across the aisle? Did you ever want to strangle the Whitney Houston-wanna-be wailing behind you?

Remember, your ticket makes you a member of the audience, not a member of the cast.

Arrive on time. Stage performers may be distracted by your unfashionably late entrance.

When the lights flash, you have two minutes to dispose of your refreshments and take your seats. Face the stage as you enter the row. Hold your coat or handbag close so you don't restyle the hairdos of those in front of you. Say, "Please excuse me" to the owners of the toes you're trying not to step on.

Silence is golden in the theater. Your rustling of the program annoys those around you. Save your stashed refreshments for intermission. And please, leave anything that beeps or jingles at home.

Your commentary doesn't make the performance any more meaningful, so save your review for the lobby. Be assured that singing along with a musical performance is not a form of applause.

The cause for applause differs from one production to another. A lull in the action does not necessarily mean you should clap. If you are unsure, wait to see what others are doing. A little hesitation may save you a lot of embarrassment.

When entertaining a client or customer, purchase the best seats possible. The days of buying "cheap seats" (and then moving to any unoccupied seats in front) are *over*.

Although the theater is dark, it is no place for dozing. Falling asleep is bad enough, but snoring is inexcusable.

Shakespeare may have asked, "to be, or not to be," but the question today is, "TO TIP, OR NOT TO TIP?"

Tipping is an acceptable, voluntary practice. The amount of the tip speaks louder than words — so let the tip do the talking! If the service was wonderful, by all means up the ante. If your service was not up to your expectations, let the management know. It is not your responsibility to reprimand anyone or just leave a penny.

The amount to leave is based on 15% to 20% of the service or the bill, *before* tax. When you are tipping for more than one service, put it in an envelope and itemize how the cash, check, or charge payment should be divided.

> " **let your tips do the talking...** "

airport shuttle driver: Do not tip.

airport skycap: Curbside check-in should be $1 per bag if you want your belongings to arrive at your destination.

bartender: 15% to 20% of your tab, but a minimum of 50¢.

bed & breakfast: You may leave a tip in your room for any of the staff (remember, never tip the owners) that serve you.

buffet staff: Tip only on the drinks you're served.

busboy: Do not tip. He shares with the wait person.

chambermaid: Depends on the length of your stay. Give her $2 to $3 per day, but either hand it to her or leave it at the front desk. Do not leave it in the room.

coat attendant: $1 per coat.

concierge: Depending on the service (getting you tickets to a play or tickets to a sold out performance), the tip can be anywhere from $3 to 10% of the ticket costs.

counter server: 15% to 20% of your bill, but a minimum of 50¢.

doorman: If he provides a service (hails you a cab), $1.

hotel shuttle driver: 15% of what a cab would cost.

limousine driver: 15% of the cost.

maître d': Only if he performs a *special* service that you have requested (leapfrogs your reservation, puts you at a preferred table ...). Then he is tipped $10 to $20 in cash after the service has been performed.

porter: Based on how many and how heavy your bags are, tip $1 to $2 per bag.

proprietors: Do not tip, but consider a gift for a special occasion sometime during the year.

rest room attendant: For handing you the towel, 50¢. If he or she provides a service, leave $1. Don't hesitate to ask if you need something.

room service: If there is a service charge already added to the bill, you may tip the delivery person $1 to $2.

salon services: 15% to 20% of each service; itemized on the bill.

taxi drivers: 15% of the charge.

valet parking attendant: When your car is returned to you, tip $2.

wait person: In a restaurant, the host (never the guest) leaves the tip. The bill should always be face down. Tip 15% to 20% of the bill.

wine steward: If you use his service, leave 15% of the cost of the wine. Itemize this on your bill.

A gratuity (generally 10%) is different from a tip because it is automatically added to your bill. Increase the amount if you want to.

Many restaurants will include the tip if there are more than six people in a party. (The bill should indicate this.) The tip is based on the amount before tax is added.

When men and women colleagues travel together, each is responsible for their own tipping.

The tradition of toasting thrives. Wedding receptions, birthday and holiday celebrations, dinners of all kinds, and many other occasions are times for a toast. Certain guidelines may be helpful for the "toaster" and the "toastee":

Give a toast at the beginning of the meal and/or before the dessert. Raise a glass of any beverage — water, soft drink, or alcohol.

If you (the "toaster") are toasting someone, don't bang your glass with your knife to get the group's attention. Simply standing with your drink raised should alert people more politely than the clanging of cutlery on glass. A prepared toast is nice, so always have one ready in case you're asked to give a toast, even if it's *"Here's to good friends,"* or *"To the cook,"* or *"Salut."* Avoid anything to the effect of, *"Over the teeth, past the gums, watch out stomach here it comes."* Not funny. This is also not your opportunity to

toasting tips:

- toast at the right time
- don't bang your glass
- always have a toast ready
- keep it short
- be original
- don't toast yourself

get in a dig, slam anyone, or reopen a debate. Get the idea?

People's hands get tired holding up a glass for more than a minute or two, which is all the longer your toast should be. Be original and your toast will mean more. The host or hostess (that's right, a woman) makes the first toast.

If you are the guest of honor, and therefore the "toastee," don't raise your glass for the toast with the rest. This is like singing happy birthday with the group before you blow out the candles. Admittedly, just sitting there and watching everyone toast to you might make you a little uncomfortable. When they are finished toasting to you, it is your turn. Stand up and say thank you.

The purpose of attending a trade show or convention is to promote your company and its products by meeting potential clients or customers. The trade show is not a non-stop business bash.

Dress professionally. Even if the trade show is at a resort, your spouse is with you, and the mariachi music is playing by the pool ... you are still there to work.

At some point, you will probably have to work the company booth. Always stand, and try to look enthusiastic. Be approachable and eager to greet people as they stop by. Encourage them to come in and look at your product. Be prepared to answer questions other than the whereabouts of the drinking fountain or rest room. Although you may be focusing on or talking to one customer, try not to ignore newcomers.

When you visit another company's booth, make sure it's because you're interested in its products and not just to collect the giveaways or have your fortune told.

This is a perfect time to exchange business cards (hint, hint).

Train travel can be pleasant, if time permits. Speaking of time, don't be late. Those exciting movie scenes of someone racing down the tracks to catch the train aren't so much fun in real life.

■ You will have to carry your own bags and seating is open.

■ Always tip the waiter in the Club or Dining Car.

■ Have your ticket ready when the conductor comes by to punch it.

■ No one watches for your stop but you, so don't sleep through it.

Traveling is one of the mainstays of the business diet. It is made up of one fourth business and three fourths down time. Get used to it. You may be traveling with a colleague, senior manager, member of the opposite sex, spouse, or by yourself. Whether you're in the air, on the sea, or on the ground, you are always a representative of your company and your travel manners are visible. (No pressure, right?)

If your company is affiliated with a travel agency or has a travel department, use it! Forget relying on your Uncle Phil's travel agent cousin who lives 600 miles away.

When two people of unequal rank travel together, the person of lesser rank gets to handle all of the details, such as getting a taxi, tipping, making reservations, picking up meal tabs, and any other way he or she can be of assistance.

You might think that this is the time to air (bad pun intended) your viewpoints about the vending machine selections or the new receptionist with your boss. Maybe and maybe not. Let the senior manager initiate a lengthy conversation with you. He or she may have ideas, none of which may include you or should come from you.

Make sure you always have plenty of dollar bills for tipping. You'll look like a rookie not having anything smaller than a fifty (or not having any cash at all).

Unless you are at a business function, don't feel obligated to socialize or spend time with your colleagues after work hours.

Pack light and carry your own luggage. It's rude to expect someone to wait for you while you check luggage tags to your look-alike mauve tapestry bag. If you forget a hair dryer or iron, the hotel will supply one, but request it in advance. To be late meeting a client because your dress needed pressing shows your travel inexperience.

When male and female colleagues travel together, each is responsible for carrying his own bags, tipping, meals, and any other expenses.

Like it or not, business travel can be a special concern for women. Make flight reservations for daylight, if possible. Avoid flirtations, no matter how innocent they may seem. If you want to have a drink in the bar, go ahead, but make sure your dress and behavior are professional.

Many women would rather pay $18 for a room service hamburger just to stay in their rooms than go to a restaurant alone. If a woman wants to have dinner in a restaurant, elegant or casual, she should! If you want to give the message that you don't want to be bothered, have something to read with you.

Bring expensive jewelry only if you plan to wear it all the time, because hotel rooms are not safe places to leave valuables.

Have identification tags with your business address on *everything,* even carry-ons.

Eat, drink, speak, and act with caution while on the road. Your claim to fame will come, but it doesn't have to be by next Thursday. Remember *travel* can get you into *trouble* — both begin with *tr.*

U tensils were made to be used. Sounds easy, until you are suddenly faced with a shining array of forks and spoons. Which one comes first? If in doubt, mimic someone else (preferably one who knows), or start from the outside of your row of utensils and work your way toward the center (your plate).

A fork is a fork, and therefore is never to be used as a spear or a shovel. Two eating styles exist, and the choice is yours.

zig zag method

Hold your fork handle in your left palm, index finger at the base, tines down in the piece of meat.
The knife handle is in your right palm, index finger at the base. Bend your wrists and keep your elbows close to your sides so you don't elbow your dinner partner.

Cut up to three pieces of meat, but don't eat it all at the same time. Place your knife in the rest position, which is horizontally across the top of your plate. The knife blade

faces you. The whole knife is on the plate, not half hanging off (gangplank style). Now transfer the fork to your right hand and bring

the food to your mouth with the tines up. Use your knife, never your fingers, if you need a pusher. If you aren't using your dinner fork, rest it on your plate.

European method

Hold your fork and knife the exact same way as the zig zag method, *EXCEPT* that you don't ever transfer the fork to your right hand. Keep it in your left hand and bring the food to your mouth with the tines down. The knife remains in your right hand close to your plate, not waved in the air.

The European rest position is similar to an "X", made with your knife and fork, tines down.

finished position

When you have finished, place your knife and fork side by side diagonally across your plate, with the knife above the fork, blade down. Fork tines are up (zig zag) or down (European). This will tell any good waiter that you're finished.

How exciting to be asked to participate in an on-camera (electronic) meeting. Be prepared, not just with your contribution to the meeting, but know the set up of the room and the dress code. Will you be in full view (living room setting) or will just your upper half be seen (around a conference table)? Will the audience be able to see those Nikes you're hiding under the table?

Video magnifies everything from clothing and makeup to gestures and speech patterns. Stick to neutral-colored clothing. Women should choose bold jewelry over anything dangling or glitzy.

Even if it's casual day, dress up. Apply makeup subtlely because that which gives a dewy look in regular lights can look spackled like Bozo the Clown on camera. Men should be clean shaven.

If more than one camera is being used, find out which one will focus on you. Face the correct camera. Sit up straight. Do not interrupt, talk too loudly, laugh obnoxiously, or gesture in your neighbor's face. Avoid doodling, yawning, and appearing bored. This is exciting!

Twitching your nose, tapping your fingers, smirking, and chewing on your pencil or eyeglass stems may not be prominent in a regular meeting; however, on camera they are magnified and viewed by a much larger audience.

Have you ever been locked in a voice mail jail? It goes like this: You call Suzy Que, who is unavailable, so you get a recording that says "Suzy Que is unavailable, but if you need immediate assistance, please press 123." So you press 123, only to find that the immediate assistance person is also unavailable, but you are told that, "if you want the weather report dial 124, or the airline schedule dial 125, or the meaning of life dial 126 ... " This continues until after about ten minutes of being shunted through electronic circuits, you get a real person who doesn't know where anyone is. Frustrating, isn't it?

Voice mail is an effective way to leave a message when the person you've called is unavailable. Sometimes a receptionist might ask if you would like to leave a voice mail message. If you choose to do this, have your reason for calling ready, and make your message brief. Always leave your telephone number since the person may be retrieving his or her messages from another location. And of course speak slowly and clearly, since it takes longer to write down a message than it does to say it.

Remember that voice mail can be transferred and shared around an office at the touch of a button. So don't leave a confidential or irate message. No matter how justified it seems at the time, your angry message *will* come back to haunt you, especially when the person receives it after things have blown over (... or so you'd thought).

Voice mail is great for intra-company communication, but can be offensive to a client or customer if used improperly. Write down your voice mail message and practice what you're going to say. Practice it until your voice sounds natural. Update your message often. Callers also appreciate having some idea when you will return the call.

It's okay to hide temporarily behind this electronic device, but you still have to return the call quickly.

orget the old rules of red wine with beef and white wine with fish or fowl. Many people like a light wine with everything, while others may prefer a heavier wine with light foods. Anything goes — with wine, that is, not behavior.

When you're the host, offer both red and white wine, unless you know everyone has the same preference. If only one person wants red, then order that person a glass of red wine.

Look beyond the labels and don't assume a wine is great just because the price is high, the name is hard to pronounce, and the label is fancy. Wine is a matter of taste.

If you have a wine connoisseur in your group, defer the decision to him or her (if your expense account can afford it).

It's always nice to be familiar with a couple of good wines (a red and a white). But what happens if you don't have a clue about wine, the wine list is the size of a dictionary, and the wine steward (who has to be tipped if you use his service) arrives? Don't hide under the table. Take the wine list and point to the price you want to spend and tell the wine steward you want something "from this area." Your guests won't know whether you're talking about region or price.

When the wine steward brings your bottle of wine to the table, he will show you the label to make sure you're getting what you ordered. After you nod with approval, he will pour a small amount in your glass. Taste it and give your approval.

A good host makes sure guests' glasses are always filled. The host may pour additional glasses of wine rather than waiting for the waiter to return. White wine should fill 3/4 of a glass, and red wine fills only 1/2 of a glass. Hold a stemmed glass by the stem.

If you don't care for any wine, simply put your finger over the glass when the waiter gets to you.

Don't take a bite out of the wine cork or sniff it, unless you know what you're sniffing for. If the wine steward hands it to you, put it on your service plate. Everyone, wine connoisseur or not, will know a bad bottle of wine. Simply tasting it will do.

A carafe of house wine may be ordered at lunch, but should be avoided for dinner.

Here are some basic terms relating to wine:

aftertaste: lingering taste of a complex wine

aroma: lingering perfume of a young wine

body: substance and weight of wine

bouquet (boo-KA): fragrance first encountered when opening or tasting a mature wine

carafe: vessel for serving wine

dry: not sweet; without added sugar

house wine: a branded wine, chosen by the restaurant, as a less costly alternative to the more expensive wines

sommelier (sum-el-yay): wine steward

a final thought

Your resume may get you an interview, but your attitude will get you the job.

"There is no accomplishment so
easy to acquire as politeness,
and none more profitable"

George Bernard Shaw